"In his book *Self-Esteem, Self-Im...* ...d-on the popular yet destructive tren... ...find meaning to life, fulfillment, and even happ... ...inced far too many people, even those in the church, that turning inward and self-focusing will provide the answers so desperately needed in life. But God's Word presents an antithetical phenomenology to secularism that is both necessary and healing. As Dr. Ellen illuminates in this important book, Scripture does not ignore that each person has a self-image. However, the Bible presents a person's self-image as intrinsically designed to flow from one's esteem for, love for, and intimate knowledge of the image of the Creator God. It is in this right covenant relationship that one can rightly discern and evaluate his/herself. This book is not only informative, but it is also practical, and I highly recommend it for counselors, pastors, small groups, teens, as well as anyone who might be struggling with identity issues. If you want a comprehensive biblical perspective on these issues, then *Self-Esteem, Self-Image, Self-Love* is for you."

Daniel R. Berger II (Ph.D.), author, speaker, biblical counselor, phenomenologist, and founder of Alethia International Ministries

"People tend to view self-love, self-esteem, and self-image as either a major insight into the human condition or a hopelessly bankrupt concept which leads to hardship and suffering. Dr. Ellen shows how both attitudes need to be refined by biblical truth. This resource explains how people can rightly view themselves according to Scripture. As an added bonus, he gives us a process to use when evaluating the truth-claims that come from secular psychology."

Rob Green (Ph.D.), pastor of Counseling and Seminary Ministries at Faith Church, Lafayette, IN, and Master of Arts in Biblical Counseling Dept. chair and instructor of Faith Bible Seminary, Lafayette, IN

"I have long appreciated and benefited from Nicolas' teaching. As expected, his treatment of this important subject is carefully explained and practically applied. I encourage every believer to pursue a solid, biblically-grounded response to all the competing 'noise' we hear from the world of what it means to understand and live out our true identity. Nicolas' book is a reliable resource for you in this matter."

Tim Keeter (M.A.), lay elder at Grace Community Church, Huntsville, AL, author of *Help! My Child is Being Bullied*, and Certified Biblical Counselor by the Association of Certified Biblical Counselors

"Where we focus our effort is vital to successful living, and at times the world redirects our focus in destructive ways. Worshiping self under the banner of 'self-esteem' has proven to be one of those ways. Nicolas Ellen provides us with a biblical refocus. He helps us think through the importance of concentrating on loving God and loving others through the power of the Holy Spirit rather than focusing on improving our self-esteem. He provides a practical way for us to evaluate our lives according to God's perspective and enjoy the satisfying life of worshiping God."

Andrew Rogers (M.Div., M.A., Ph.D. Candidate), executive director, Overseas Instruction in Counseling, and board member of the Association of Certified Biblical Counselors

"Dr. Nicolas Ellen is a loving and effective communicator who has written a gem for every Christian on an often misunderstood subject of self-esteem, self-image, and self-love. Dr. Ellen clearly and biblically defines this issue and its elements for anyone seeking to gain God's perspective on this topic. It is a vital issue for the addicted and their family members. This book will be a valuable resource for each person I am privileged to counsel and I recommend you add it to your biblical resource list, too."

Mark E. Shaw (D. Min.), author of *The Heart of Addiction* and 21 other resources, and founder of The Addiction Connection (www.theaddictionconnection.org)

"My friend Dr. Nicolas Ellen has served Christ's church well by writing this important book on Self-Love and Self-Image. Because Nicolas is a careful theologian, the book is filled with biblical truth. Because he is a seasoned pastor and biblical counselor, the book is filled with practical, life-changing application. And because Nicolas loves Jesus, the book is filled with the gospel of grace. I heartily recommend this book to biblical counselors and all those who seek to faithfully follow the Lord."

Steve Viars (D.Min.), senior pastor, Faith Church in Lafayette, IN, and board member of the Association of Certified Biblical Counselors and of the Biblical Counseling Coalition

SELF-ESTEEM
SELF-IMAGE
SELF-LOVE

How to Trade the Trinity of Self-Worship
for the Triangle of Self-Evaluation

NICOLAS ANDRÉ ELLEN

Expository Counseling Training Center

Houston, Texas

Book Cataloging Data
Ellen, Nicolas André
Self-Esteem, Self-Image, Self-Love : how to trade the trinity of
    self-worship for the triangle of self-evaluation
Includes bibliographical references
ISBN 978-1-952902-00-0 (pbk.)
ISBN 978-1-952902-01-7 (eBook)
1. Biblical Counseling 2. Christian Living 3. Self-Esteem

Published by Expository Counseling Training Center
Houston, Texas

https://MyCounselingCorner.com

To my dear wife
Venessa
I love you and thank you

Contents

Acknowledgments

I am truly amazed at the grace of God; He has blessed me in so many ways.

He allowed me to marry my beautiful wife, Dr. Venessa Yvette Ellen. I truly appreciate her love, care, patience, and wise counsel.

Thank you to my daughters Venezia and Lindsey; my grandchildren Jeremiah, Blake, Elijah, and Andrew; my parents Irvin and Thelma, and my in-laws Doug and Linda. They have given me their love, support, and encouragement.

God also put so many people around me who inspired and helped me. I would especially like to thank the following.

My dissertation advisor, Dr. John Babler, took the time to mentor and direct me. His guidance also aided me in developing this book.

Rich Thomson has been my friend and mentor for over twenty years. He taught me the importance of proper exegesis and exposition of Scripture, along with the proper exegesis and exposition of people's hearts through the Scripture. He has truly been instrumental in my passion for and practice in biblical counseling.

Randy Patten has given me clear instructions, as well as ample opportunities, to put into practice many of the truths discussed in this book. His accountability, prayers, and wisdom have helped me throughout the years.

Dr. Stuart Scott and Dr. John Street have been my mentors for well over twenty years. Their wise counsel and guidance have helped me develop in the art and ministry of biblical counseling.

Karen Medlin and Barbara Werden have been such a blessing in editing, organizing, and designing my manuscript to make this book's message clear and concise. I look forward to doing more writing with you.

Finally, I will be forever grateful for the prayers and support of my church family and friends. Thank you for giving me time to write and sharing me with the world.

SELF-ESTEEM
SELF-IMAGE
SELF-LOVE

Introduction

JOHN WILSON'S THOUGHTS RACE AND COLLIDE. *I can't believe it! He is saying he's proud of the progress I'm making.* John blinks and tries to focus on Pastor Smith, seated across from him.

The pastor continues with a smile, "Yes, John. In the past two weeks of counseling, you have really made strong efforts in recognizing some major sin issues. You're saying you're ready to work on them, and I believe with God's help, you will make great strides."

John sighs in relief, but almost immediately his mind begins to combat the pastor's encouragement. *He's probably just trying to keep me coming to counseling. I'll bet he sees so much wrong with me that he thinks he has to pat me on the back, just to buck up my courage.*

John stammers a reply, "Thanks, Pastor . . . I appreciate your kind words and how you're opening up God's Word to me. I'm starting to see the ways it applies to where I'm struggling. But I have to admit," with a quick breath and throat-clearing, "I somehow don't truly believe that I'm capable of changing. Some days I get up feeling so discouraged, and . . . well, useless. When anyone tells me anything that's positive about myself, it just rolls off. But the criticism? Oh, boy—I mull that over for days. It seems to confirm what I think and feel: that I don't love myself and maybe even hate myself! Guess that sounds crazy? But it's true."

How should Pastor Smith handle this? Should he commiserate with John and just listen? Should he challenge John's ideas about self-esteem? Maybe he should help John see that focusing on himself can equate to self-worship. How would you handle this if you were counseling John?

Is there any validity to the concepts of self-esteem, self-image, or self-love? Does the Bible have anything to say about these issues? In some Christian circles, the ideas of self-esteem, self-image, and self-love are seen as evil, ungodly, and unmentionable among fellow Christians. They may assert, "The Bible says in 2 Timothy 3:1 that difficult times will come because men will be lovers of themselves. So how can we even think to embrace concepts like self-esteem, self-image, or self-love?" However, other Christians have attempted to integrate concepts of secular humanistic self-esteem, self-image, and self-love with Christian principles and Scriptures. Therefore, you may hear statements such as "We cannot learn to love others until first learning to love ourselves."

Who is right? Maybe there is a different perspective altogether. What if self-esteem, self-image, and self-love are not synonymous? In other words, perhaps these concepts are related but not the same? What if the secular perspectives of self-esteem, self-image, or self-love are completely antithetical to a biblical framework of self? Is it possible that the Bible provides an alternative to the humanistic perspectives of self-esteem, self-image, and self-love?

The psychological construct of self-esteem has been a significant issue in the overall United States culture, throughout the field of psychology, and within Christian culture and local churches. While this concept is still debated today, its prominence has far-reaching effects, such as influencing judicial decisions and being used to explain issues faced in romantic relationships. The study and use of self-esteem by various theorists have impacted the way people see and evaluate themselves. However, humanistic psychology through its definitions and models of self-esteem contradicts God's view of man, revealing an unbiblical view of self, a preoccupation with self, and a rejection of the reality of man's being a sinner in need of God.

In this book we will uncover how secular self-esteem concepts filtered into our culture in the twentieth and twenty-first centuries.

We will highlight the views of man that permeate these concepts and oppose a biblical understanding of self. We will also see the Bible's idea of self and contrast that framework with the secular views of self-esteem, demonstrating that these frameworks are incompatible.

But we can take heart! We will discover a biblical approach to self-esteem, self-image, and self-love. This approach can help us trade the trinity of self-worship for the triangle of self-evaluation. In other words, we will learn how to gain a biblical perspective of self-esteem, self-image and self-love in order to evaluate ourselves to see where we are sinning against God and others or where we are walking in love for God and love for others.

Here are the central points we will consider:

- Secular self-esteem is incompatible to a biblical framework of self.

- A biblical framework of self can lead and enable us to disregard secular self-esteem theories in our daily lives.

- A biblical framework of self can lead us to distinguish self-esteem, self-image, and self-love from each other.

- Self-esteem from a biblical perspective highlights the conscience's ability to produce peace or guilt according to right or wrong choices, thereby leading us to feel good or bad about ourselves.

- Self-image from a biblical perspective highlights the concepts of pride and humility: it demonstrates that one's self-image is either based on truth resulting in humility or error resulting in pride.

- Self-love from a biblical perspective shows that self-love has three basic categories presented in Scripture: selfish self-love (2 Tim. 3:1-5), self-preserving self-love (Eph. 5:28-30), and soul-loving self-love (Prov. 19:8). Therefore, our love for self is either neutral, wise, or evil—depending on the context.

Are you curious? Are you skeptical? Good! Please read this book to see if it delivers on what it promises. May this book be used as a redemptive tool in individual lives, leading to transformation of souls into the image of Jesus Christ.

Chapter 1

HISTORY, UNDERSTANDING, AND USE OF THE CONCEPT OF SELF-ESTEEM

L ET'S TAKE A JOURNEY to examine the history of the concept of self-esteem, key definitions of self-esteem used in the U.S. culture, and some theories and implications of self-esteem as understood in the culture. We will bring to light a clear understanding of secular self-esteem, as well as its implications.

An insightful writer named E. Brooks Holifield believed that humans have moved from self-denial to self-love, from self-love to self-culture, from self-culture to self-mastery, and from self-mastery to self-realization. This preoccupation with self has paved the way for theorists in the field of psychology to become very interested in the concept of self-esteem. In fact, secular self-esteem theories keep a person focused on him- or herself. A later chapter will contrast secular self-esteem with a biblical understanding and framework of self.

THE HISTORY OF THE CONCEPT OF SELF-ESTEEM

The term *self-esteem* can be traced back as far as the 1600s; its use reached a peak around the 1800s and then for seventy-five years was not widely mentioned. As the study of psychology became more popular in the 1960s and 1970s, five central theories began to take form:

1. The ratio of achievement and expectation
2. Positive and negative self-regard
3. Inferiority complex
4. The impact of human relationships on one's view of self
5. Attachment theory.

The ratio of achievement and expectation theory suggests that a person's opinion of himself is directly related to how well he meets his own expectations. The positive and negative self-regard theory presents the idea that for a person to overcome the outrageous demands and judgments from within and thus to function well in society, he must develop a positive view of himself. The inferiority complex theory suggests that a person will experience a sense of inadequacy as a result of not reaching some desired goal. The human relationship theory asserts that a person's conflict with others may lead him to fight, comply, or be aloof, impacting how he views himself. Finally, attachment theory asserts that a child must have a close, intimate bond with his mother during childhood to avoid irreversible mental health consequences, which may eventually lead to problems with attachment to others.

These theories were simplified by explaining them through the concept of self-esteem. They notably focus on one's view of oneself, without any biblical context.

In short, these theories assert that a person's view of himself, his goals for himself, along with how others view and treat him, are the sum total of his existence. He is defined by his own view of himself and the opinions of others, not by God and God's description of humanity. These factors determine whether he succeeds or fails in life. As a result, we hear others exhort us to "Believe in yourself," "Follow your heart," "Trust yourself," "Listen to your gut," or "I believe in you, so believe in yourself."

Have you seen the films *The Wizard of Oz* or the African American version called *The Wiz*? As Dorothy and the crew go on a fascinating journey in search of this great Wizard to give them something of value to themselves, they discover something very special. What they need from the Wizard or Wiz is already inside themselves. Through the support of each other, they could find the answers within themselves. When we evaluate secular self-esteem concepts and theories, we ultimately discover the same message behind them. According to these theories, what we need is already within ourselves, and with the help of others we can find it. Just like *The Wizard of Oz* or *The Wiz*, we will find that these theories are based on much fantasy.

THE HUMAN POTENTIAL MOVEMENT'S IMPACT ON THE CONCEPT OF SELF-ESTEEM

The self-esteem movement further grew in popularity through the "Human Potential Movement" in the 1960s and 1970s. The Human Potential Movement influenced individuals to pursue the realization of their inner human potential through exploration of their body and mind. This movement gained popularity as it focused on fulfilling and gratifying inner personal longings to gain individual identity and meaning. It was therefore an attempt to foster the feelings of power, self-esteem, and happiness in people without truly modifying the real conditions of life. Abraham Maslow, Rollo May, and Carl Rogers promoted and advanced the Human Potential Movement by connecting human dignity and self-actualization to self-esteem.

Human dignity theory presents the idea that individuals have inherent value or worth and deserve to be treated accordingly. The self-actualization theory suggests that a person can become fully human or mature by striving to become all he can be. It is fascinating how these theories center on a person's pursuit to define or redefine himself, apart from considering the obvious reality that no one has created himself and cannot truly define or redefine himself apart from guidance from the Creator.

When a person leaves God out of the equation, he is left to his own devices. When left to his own devices, he will choose to create his own meaning and purpose. This results in redefining his reason for existence and redefining relationships to fit his own meaning and purpose. This leads to further folly and confusion in life as the person seeks to reach his potential according to standards he alone has established.

If you do not know where you are going, then any trail will get you there. The Human Potential Movement is a perfect example of what happens when people choose to "wing it" instead of embracing the reality and will of God. I had a friend who would say to me, "Well, I just make up stuff when I don't know what to do." He struggled so much in his life. So will we if we buy into these ideas.

One of the first to advocate for the Human Potential Movement was Abraham Maslow. Maslow is considered one of the most important American psychologists. He served as the psychology department chair at Brandeis University from 1951 to 1961. During the 1940s and 1950s, he developed a theory of motivation in which he explained how people could move from basic needs such as food and water, to their need of self-esteem, and finally to their ultimate need of self-actualization. This theory came to be known as Maslow's Hierarchy of Needs.

Rollo May was a prominent existential psychologist, therapist, and psychoanalyst from the 1950s to the 1980s. He believed that individuals experience significance as a sense of power. May also believed that part of one's journey to self-maturity requires maintaining self-esteem.

Carl Rogers is known as the developer of "person-centered counseling," which promotes the idea that individuals possess the answers within themselves to fix their own problems. Rogers asserted that humans have inherent goodness and can self-actualize in the right environment. He also believed that once a person learns to love, respect, and accept himself, he can begin to self-actualize.

According to the Human Potential Movement, a person is at the center of her existence, inherently good, and able to determine her destiny, apart from any need of God. This theory obviously evaluates people separated from a biblical framework. When sin is not the problem, then Jesus Christ is not the answer. What is our alternative to Him? Self-esteem and self-actualization become our alternative.

Imagine you are put in a situation where someone tells you that you only have two hard choices. The choices are either dying slowly from taking poison or dying quickly by being shot. Which would you choose?

Before you answer the question, consider this possibility. The one giving you the alternatives may be limiting your choices because you are not aware of other alternatives. When a person limits himself to himself alone, he is choosing to die either a slow death or quick death. The Bible says that he who trusts in his own heart is a fool, but he who walks wisely will be delivered (Prov. 28:26). The Bible also says cursed is the man who puts confidence in flesh (Jer. 17:5). We did not create ourselves. Therefore, to put confidence in ourselves or in others limits us to the abilities and disabilities of ourselves and others, leading to our own demise. However, we will discover as we study further that human life is not limited to self-esteem and self-actualization.

IDEAS ABOUT SELF-ESTEEM FROM THE
1980S TO TODAY

From the 1980s to the 1990s, the California Task Force to Promote Self-Esteem and Personal and Social Responsibility wielded significant influence within the United States. Its members promoted the idea that self-esteem could play an important role in mitigating social ills such as poverty, drug use, and premarital sex. This organization produced various studies and books and collaborated with the California state government to facilitate the members' agenda. According to this organization, people with high self-esteem are more productive citizens than people with low self-esteem.

The California Task Force regarded self-esteem as the key to people's problems and solutions both personally and socially, without considering a biblical context. Again, individuals are seen as the source and solution to their own problems. How can a person be both source and solution to his own problems? How can a person be her own problem and also be her own savior? According to this Task Force, a person holds his own solution, and self-esteem is his formula to heal himself.

Sometimes when I am with my wife, I believe I know where we are going and the best way to get there. If we get lost, I don't like asking for directions. We have a GPS, but of course I want to figure it out myself, because I believe I have the answer within me. I need the help of someone who has more insights to guide me in the right direction, but I get consumed with my own answers. So it is with us as humans, whether child or adult. We need more than our own self-esteem and other self-contained solutions to get us out of the problems we have today. We need the GPS system of life, God Himself.

Since 2000, the concept of self-esteem has been evaluated, studied, and promoted through the field of positive psychology, which evaluates self-esteem according to its impact on life satisfaction, dissatisfaction, and productivity. Positive psychology also builds upon the ideas of humanistic psychology, which focuses on the positive perspectives of human beings over the negative. In addition, positive psychology studies the correlation between optimism, self-esteem, gratefulness, and one's sense of well-being.

Positive psychology focuses on self-esteem as the underlying foundation to a person's well-being and without considering a biblical context. So in essence, the person who did not create himself seeks to study and come up with solutions that will help himself maintain well-being. As a result, he believes that self-esteem is the answer.

What do you think would happen if you were to leave your young child to come up with what is necessary to maintain his or her well-being? Would she be able to find healthy food to eat, arrange transportation to school, or deal with any emergencies that occur? Self-esteem is what happens when you leave human beings to develop their well-being apart from their Creator.

In summary, the five central theories encompassed by the term *self-esteem*, the Human Potential Movement and theorists that developed it, the California Task Force to Promote Self-Esteem and Personal and Social Responsibility, and positive psychology have a common focus. All emphasize self-esteem's impact on people's well-being, without taking into account a biblical context.

DEFINITIONS OF SELF-ESTEEM USED IN OUR CULTURE

From the 1800s to the late 1980s, several key scholars such as William James, Robert White, Morris Rosenberg, Stanley Coopersmith, Nathaniel Branden, Christopher J. Mruk, and Seymour Epstein developed foundational definitions of *self-esteem* that have influenced other researchers. William James, Robert White, and Christopher J.

Mruk defined *self-esteem* in terms of one's positive or negative feelings about one's self as the result of accomplishing or not accomplishing certain tasks. In contrast, Nathaniel Branden, Stanley Coopersmith, and Morris Rosenberg defined *self-esteem* in terms of one's evaluation of self as positive or negative, apart from accomplishing or not accomplishing a task. However, Seymour Epstein's approach was different from both camps by describing self-esteem as the need to be love-worthy. Let's look at each theorist's definition individually.

William James was a key developer of the philosophy known as pragmatism. He taught his first psychology course in 1875 at Harvard. In 1890, James defined *self-esteem* as a ratio between what one aspires to do and what one actually accomplishes. In other words, the way a person feels about himself is determined by what he does in relation to his abilities.

Robert White, another Harvard psychologist, was noted for creating a clear and articulate insight into the expression of self-esteem. In 1963, White defined *self-esteem* as the product of one's ability to master certain aspects according to one's identity, resulting in the pleasure of feeling good about one's self.

Morris Rosenberg was a sociologist who produced the Rosenberg Self-Esteem Scale. He also helped to reintroduce the term *self-esteem* to mainstream American culture in the early 1960s. In 1965, Rosenberg defined *self-esteem* as satisfaction or dissatisfaction with oneself. If a person feels he has worth, his self-esteem is high; if he feels unworthy, he has low self-esteem.

Stanley Coopersmith was a student of Abraham Maslow and a professor at the University of California. He examined the need for self-esteem through a ten-year study in the U.S. of middle-class boys aged six to twelve. He produced a popular book on his findings called *The Antecedents of Self-Esteem*. In 1967, Coopersmith defined *self-esteem* as the evaluation of a person's worth, which is revealed in his attitudes toward himself, whether approval or disapproval. Accord-

SELF-ESTEEM, SELF-IMAGE, SELF-LOVE

ing to Coopersmith, self-esteem is a subjective appraisal of one's worth.

Nathaniel Branden, also known for his partnership with author and existentialist philosopher Ayn Rand, contributed to the self-esteem movement primarily through his book *The Six Pillars of Self-Esteem*. In 1969, Branden defined *self-esteem* as "the disposition to experience oneself as competent to cope with the basic challenges of life and as worthy of happiness."

Christopher J. Mruk is professor of psychology at Bowling Green State University. Over the years, Mruk balanced the research of self-esteem with clinical wisdom gained through his own research and studies. His book *Self-Esteem and Positive Psychology* is now in its fourth edition. In 1981, Mruk defined *self-esteem* as having a view of oneself as competent, as a result of dealing with the challenges of life in a productive way.

In 1973, Seymour Epstein, professor emeritus at the University of Massachusetts, was the first to introduce a global theory of personality in the field of cognitive psychology, called the "cognitive experiential self-theory." Epstein believed that self-esteem held an important place within cognitive experiential self-theory. In 1985, he defined *self-esteem* as one's basic need to be love-worthy. Epstein's definition of *self-esteem* does not correlate with any other theorist's definition. Epstein described self-esteem as the need to be love-worthy without any connection to a cause or effect idea.

In addition to these key definitions, terms such as *global self-esteem, specific self-esteem,* and *episodic self-esteem* were created to describe one's attitude toward self in connection to how one interprets a situation. Terms such as *implicit self-esteem, explicit self-esteem, state-self-esteem,* or *trait self-esteem* have also been used to explain the same idea with some variations.

In these key definitions, a person's view of herself apart from a biblical context is a consistent pattern. A person feels good or bad about himself or has a sense of his greatness or ineptness by how he identifies with the culture or how the culture identifies with him. Therefore, his evaluation of himself is left to his own ideas or the ideas of others.

Without an objective standard by which to measure reality, we can create ideas about ourselves that can lead to our misperceptions, embarrassment, or even demise. Have you ever watched the TV show "American Idol" (that title alone should tell us something)? Some people who appear on that show do objectively have wonderful singing voices. However, other contestants believe in error that they have the ability to sing beautifully. How did they come to this conclusion? They listened to themselves, believed in themselves, and received validation from others who believed in them as well.

Then these "great" singers perform for the judges and are sincerely shocked, angry, and hurt when those judges tell them how terrible they sound. Profanity and angry tirades spew forth, as these would-be singers react because the judges did not validate their false beliefs about themselves. In a similar way, many people buy into the secular self-esteem model, falling into the fallacy of measuring themselves by their own desires and beliefs. However, the truth about who they really are is reality now and will eventually be fully revealed in the presence of God.

IMPLICATIONS OF SELF-ESTEEM THEORIES
IN OUR CULTURE

As scholars and researchers sought to understand and evaluate the concept of self over the years, the meaning of the term *self-esteem* evolved. Overall, the various definitions and understandings describe self-esteem as a mental evaluation of self that is either a motivator or a by-product of one's behavior, thereby producing positive or negative perceptions, attitudes, emotional states, or feelings. Seeing self-esteem as a force behind behavior has led to definitions and theories that focus on how self-esteem can be a motivator for other concerns of life. Conversely, seeing self-esteem as a by-product of behavior has led to definitions and theories that focus on the way one derives or maintains a level of self-esteem.

Consider how this works in the secular way of thinking. Some say if you want to understand why people act the way they do, check out their self-esteem, which determines their behavior. Others say if you want to understand self-esteem, check out the way people behave, which determines their self-esteem. So the ancient philosophical question arises: Which comes first, the chicken or the egg? How can something be the motivator and the by-product at the same time? Here we can start seeing inconsistencies within the secular theory of self-esteem.

I have had some very cheap cars in my life. When one of those cars developed problems, I had to determine the source of the shaking, coughing, or thunking in order to keep it running well. Sometimes when working on a car, I thought the alternator was the problem when it was really the battery cable. Other times I thought it was the battery cable, but it really was the alternator. One thing for sure is that these were separate issues. The battery could not be both the source and the by-product of the problem. The alternator could not be the source and by-product of the problem. So it is with the theory of self-esteem: it cannot be both the by-product of behavior and the motivator of behavior at the same time.

Most self-esteem theorists would conclude that self-esteem has either a positive or negative effect on well-being and should be considered an important factor. Overall, self-esteem is theorized to have far-reaching effects, ranging from influencing body appreciation to the reason for marriage or even abortion. The study and application of self-esteem has significantly influenced our society's understanding of self.

However, these theorists and theories do not mention or present any biblical factors as relevant to man's well-being. In other words, man's well-being is not determined by how he has handled his sin before the presence of God but instead how his self-esteem is handled within himself. Therefore, sin is not the problem, Christ is not the answer, and self-esteem is the solution or the problem.

SUMMARY

Self-esteem is an amalgamation of many theories that keep humans focused on evaluating and developing themselves apart from any biblical considerations. Therefore, according to self-esteem theories mentioned in this chapter, a person's view of himself or feelings about himself are of vital importance to his well-being. This keeps a person focused on himself rather than on God. Understanding this truth enables us to examine where Christians are being led to focus on self to the exclusion of God as they embrace secular self-esteem models.

Chapter 2

A BIBLICAL FRAMEWORK OF SELF

HOW DO WE KNOW that secular self-esteem theories are not the way Christians should view themselves? Does God give us an alternate template in the Bible? With gratitude to Him, we can say Yes!

From the beginning of creation, God had order, structure, and process for humans to follow. He gave to Adam (the first man) his work, a warning, and then the first woman, Eve (Gen. 2:1-24). God's order, structure, and process are revealed throughout Scripture, and His plan for us is that these truths should shape our theology of who He is and who we are. According to Sinclair Ferguson, it is God who begins, controls, and shapes all aspects of the Christian life (1 Pet. 5:10). Therefore, the pursuit to know, reflect, and serve God is all empowered by God. Christians are to work out their calling as God works within their hearts (Phil. 2:12-13). Christians are not left to their own knowledge and strength in this great calling of God.

John MacArthur explains that no one is inherently qualified to serve as a disciple of Jesus Christ (Rom. 3:10-23). Everyone who is to know God, become like God, and serve God must be born again in Jesus Christ (John 3:1-18). As a result, one cannot work out what has not first been provided through the power of God. So no one can boast of ability to serve, since it is all granted by God (Eph. 2:8-10).

The result, as Tim Chester explained, is that Christians are accepted by God so they can change. God gives Christians a new identity in Him, making them new creatures in Jesus Christ (2 Cor. 5:17). Christians have abilities He grants to know, reflect, and serve God (Rom. 6:1-7:6). Therefore, Christians do not need to depend upon their own power, or secular humanistic ideas such as self-esteem, to fulfill their God-given calling. Christians need to walk by the Spirit of God to fulfill their calling (Gal. 5:1-23).

Writing from a similar perspective, John Koessler presents the idea of spiritual development as being not so much what one does as much as an outgrowth of who one is in Jesus Christ. In other words, a person pursues knowing, reflecting, and serving God because of his identity in Jesus Christ. Consequently, as he identifies with Jesus Christ, he will pursue his calling in Jesus Christ. Embracing his identity in Christ should lead to his spiritual development in God the Son, separate from secular humanistic ideas of self-esteem.

This chapter will provide a general biblical framework of self, and this section will give a general overview of six key perspectives. These include three key Scriptures that challenge the secular humanistic self-esteem concepts, a basic understanding of what it means to be created in the image of God, an overview of the nature of humans, an overview of humanity's Fall, an overview of humanity's redemption through the Person and work of Jesus Christ, and an overview of God's agenda for humanity.

INSIGHTS ON HUMANITY AS SEEN IN THE OLD AND NEW TESTAMENTS

The Bible offers many insights about our humanness, starting from the Old Testament and continuing throughout the New Testament. However, three key biblical insights highlight the antithetical nature of Scripture to the secular humanist theories of self-esteem.

As explained earlier, self-esteem exposes a preoccupation with self-reliance, self-confidence, and self-actualization as a person's central focus of existence. Ecclesiastes 9:1, Jeremiah 10:23, and Matthew 4:4 are crucial passages that focus on these concepts, thereby demonstrating an incompatibility of secular self-esteem theories with a biblical framework of self.

First, according to Ecclesiastes 9:1, God has control over all people, and His providence means that a person cannot determine how people and circumstances will impact his life. A person's nature as a created being gives him the freedom to choose but not the control over the outcome of his choices, others' choices, or challenges that arise from people and circumstances. Therefore, a person cannot determine the outcome of his existence; only God can.

I remember hearing a pastor say in a sermon that God will let you set sail but you cannot control the weather. Although we have freedom to make choices, God determines the outcome of our choices. Therefore, we must look to God and not ourselves to determine our future.

Second, Jeremiah 10:23 states that a man's way is not his own; it cannot be determined by looking within or by trying to guide himself through life. This verse clearly asserts a person's need for God's guidance. Consequently, a person does not control her own destiny; God exercises complete authority over people. Given the assertions from these texts, one can conclude that a person cannot guide him- or herself into the destiny he/she has determined, unless that destiny is determined by God (Prov. 16:1, 9). Furthermore, a person cannot have an accurate assessment of himself, his situation, and what he is to do, apart from the God of Scripture's insight into these matters (Gen. 50:20; Rom. 12:2-3).

Third, Matthew 4:4 states that the Word of God is the food of life, the power source by which a person is meant to sustain and function in her existence as prescribed by God. Therefore, without adherence to the Word of God, a person will not be able to operate according to the purpose for which she was created. Physical food cannot provide a person with what she needs to live the kind of life intended for her existence.

In summary, Ecclesiastes 9:1, Jeremiah 10:23, and Matthew 4:4 give us a view of God as Sovereign Ruler, Sustainer, and Director of humanity in all aspects of our existence. However, the concept of self-esteem gives us a view of people as the rulers, sustainers, and directors of our own lives in all aspects of existence. These two perspectives completely contradict each other. The concepts of self-esteem lead one to focus and trust in self, whereas the Scriptures highlight the importance of depending on and trusting in God. The rest of this chapter will present a view of mankind distinctly different from that of secular humanistic self-esteem.

CREATED IN THE IMAGE OF GOD

The Bible declares that humans were created by God (Gen. 1:26-27). Yet, in presenting this point, the Bible makes the distinction that humans were created in the *image* of God. Precisely what it means to be created in the image of God is not clearly defined but stated as fact, leaving theologians to discuss (and sometimes disagree on) the exact meaning. However, it is implied to be connected to the non-physical, relational, moral, and responsibility aspects of humans. At a minimum we can understand the explanation of our being created in the image of God as distinguishing us from the rest of God's creation.

The explanation of being created in God's image can be understood as emphasizing human dignity and the resulting expectation that human life will be respected and not destroyed. Consequently, the explanation of people's being created in the image of God could simply mean that each person is intended to live and relate with God and others, while reflecting the character of his Creator God.

Theologians have therefore deduced that being created in the image of God results in humans as thinking/feeling beings, having self-consciousness, reason, and desire in the likeness of their Creator. Theologians also understand it as humans' being created with a god-likeness in mind and will, in order to carry out the express desires and decrees of God while reflecting His character. Being made in the image of God suggests that people are created as relational beings with social and dominion responsibilities.

When a manufacturer produces an item—let's say a widget—the general goal is to produce as many widgets as possible to make as much profit as possible. Therefore, great care is taken when reproducing the widgets. And how much more care our Creator God took in making us. We are created in the image of God!

Humans were not created in their own image but in God's image. Humans were not designed to determine what each person wants to be but to work toward reflecting what she was created to be. As a result, a person is not left to reflect what she thinks is best for herself but to reflect something beyond herself: the character of God. To seek to function outside of how a person was created to function is rebellion against God (Eccl. 8:11). Therefore, what a person thinks of herself is not as important as what she was commanded to think of herself (Rom. 12:2-3). In addition, people were designed to function according to duties designed and given them by God (Gen. 1:26–2:24).

Humans were created to have rule over everything created. However, people were not to put themselves first in anything. They were created to rule under the authority of God, not in autonomy apart from God.

Imagine you are the owner of a store, and you leave exact instructions with the manager about how you want your shop to operate. Yet the manager decides to run the store as his own according to his plans. Would that work for you? God left us with directions about how He wants things done and how we are to conduct ourselves. Since we were created by Him and for Him, do we have the right to live our lives and run this world as we see fit? Can we decide whom we want to be, or has that been decided for us?

HUMAN NATURE

When God created humans, he made male and female distinct from all other creation (Gen. 1:26-27). God took the ground and with His breath of life created the first man (Gen. 2:7). From this we see that each person has two aspects, both material and nonphysical, to his nature.

People's nonphysical aspect consists of mind, conscience, will, desires, and emotions. Throughout Scripture the words *heart, soul,* or *spirit* have been used to discuss any and all of these facets. Therefore, we will focus on those particular facets of mind, conscience, will, desires, and emotions in reference to the nonphysical parts of humanity.

The mind is the facet of a person's nonphysical nature by which she is able to understand or grasp meaning (Eccl. 1:16). The Scripture reveals that the mind is where a person discovers or becomes aware of things (Ps. 73:16-17). The mind defines and sets forth the meaning of things (John 4:19). In addition, Scripture states that the mind deliberates and discerns things, resulting in a person's carefully considering details and distinguishing, recognizing, and identifying things (Prov. 24:30-32; Heb. 5:14).

God also shaped the minds of humans to desire and to devise plans (Eph. 2:1-3; Prov. 16:1, 9), to make decisions, and to dream

(Luke 16:3-4; Dan. 4:5). These basic practices are important to grasp in order to think biblically about the mind.

Scripture makes it clear that human actions are determined by the inclinations of a person's mind, whether good or evil (Luke 6:45). Furthermore, the state of the person's mind is decided by what controls the mind (Rom. 8:5-8). This passage in Romans gives two examples. The person whose mind is dominated by evil will then practice evil deeds. However, the person whose mind is directed by the Holy Spirit will practice godly deeds.

We can see that the person whose mind is deceived by the devil will be blinded to the truth of the gospel and not be able to see things according to God's perspective (2 Cor. 4:3-4). But the person whose mind is delivered by the truth will have power to make proper value judgments and to be spiritually discerning of good and evil, right and wrong, and even good compared with best (1 Cor. 2:6-16). In fact, the person who is double-minded will live an unstable life because he knows the truth but lives as if he does not know (Jas. 1:5-8). We can conclude that the person whose mind is developed in the truth would be able to know the will of God as revealed in God's Word (Rom. 12:2).

Years ago a now-iconic TV commercial would end with this statement: "A mind is a terrible thing to waste." It pointed to the dangers of not giving capable people the opportunity to pursue higher education. But Scripture confronts us with the truth that a mind not centered on the purposes, precepts, and plans of God will be wasted on a culture corrupted by evil desires and doctrines of demons. This will lead to following belief systems and agendas that are antithetical to the will of God, such as secular self-esteem concepts.

As a result, the inclinations of a person's mind are carried out by the will of that person (Deut. 30:19; Josh. 24:15; Ps. 25:12). The will of a person carries out evil or good. Whatever is most influential on the person's mind, the will executes. Consequently, if he is led by the Spirit of God, the will carries out the things demonstrating that he is led by the Spirit (Rom. 8:5-7). On the other hand, if a person is led by evil, the will carries out the things that demonstrate it. In summary, the will carries out whatever dominates the mind of man (Rom. 8:5-7).

Basically, whoever or whatever controls our minds controls our decisions. We must ask ourselves this question: Who or what is controlling my thinking? How has that been displayed in my decision-making and actions? I remember years ago when a student verbally attacked me in class. He defamed my character and challenged me to a fight right there in the classroom. This man was so dominated by anger that he wanted to work it out on me. Ironically he claimed to be an anger-management therapist!

According to Romans 2:14-15, we have a conscience that accuses us when we do wrong and excuses us when we do right. God challenged Cain with the idea that if he did what is right he would feel right, implying that if Cain did wrong he would feel bad (Gen. 4:1-7). Both of these passages reveal that humans have a conscience, the innate faculty in the nonphysical aspect of a human that judges him as right or wrong in all he thinks, says, and does. This conscience makes a person aware that he is responsible to God and accountable to God for the right he is to do and the wrong he has done, resulting in a sense of pleasantness or unpleasantness in the heart (1 Sam. 24:1-15; 2 Sam. 24:10; 1 John 3:21). Consequently, we are not left to ourselves to ascertain how we should think about or function in life.

Therefore, if a person functions in a way that is not right, he or she can expect to experience the unpleasantness in the soul that comes from the conscience (Rom. 13:1-5). However, if a person functions in a way that is right, he or she can expect to experience the pleasantness in the soul that comes from the conscience (Rom. 9:1). The state of unpleasantness and pleasantness in our souls is not tied to our being worthy or unworthy but to our being guilty or clear of sin before the presence of God (Gen. 4:1-7; Rom. 2:4-14; 1 John 3:21).

Let's think about this for a moment. Whether you feel worthy or not, if you do something that is wrong in the sight of God, you experience unpleasantness in your soul. However, if you do something right in the sight of God, you experience pleasantness in your soul. These experiences are not based on your view of yourself but on your choices to do right or wrong. This truth does not line up with secular theories that we hear in relation to self-esteem.

God has also created each person's heart with emotions: the feelings that he encounters within his nonphysical and material natures that stir him to action. In addition to a person's thoughts and desires, emotions are experienced as feelings that reveal and stir him to act on what he thinks and desires. For example, the mind thinks, then the person has emotions related to what he is thinking, and then the will carries out the thoughts and emotions—unless the mind intervenes and says no (Ps. 105:25; Lev. 19:17; Eccl. 7:9, 11:10; Prov. 23:17; Deut. 28:67; John 16:6; Rom. 9:2; Acts 5:33; Matt. 5:44). Moreover, when his conscience bears witness to his mind about his doing good or evil, he experiences the emotion of the facts given by the conscience to the mind, leading to his being stirred to action (1 Sam. 24:1-15; 2 Sam. 24:10; Acts 2:37-41, 23:1).

In summary, emotions reveal the thoughts and desires within the nonphysical aspect of a person while stirring her to action. Emotions are a window to discern what a person is thinking and desiring. In addition, emotions are a motivator to an action as it is given permission by the mind and carried out by the will.

This process has huge implications in our lives. Our emotions are not random. They are connected to thoughts happening in our minds. Our emotions reveal our thoughts. Therefore, whoever or whatever controls our minds impacts our emotions.

Within the nonphysical aspect of a person, he has desires. Desires can be described as wants, longings, aspirations, or wishes for something that a person would like to have or experience. Scripture describes three categories of desires.

1. Natural desires are the normal wants or longings that correspond to the physical body (1 Cor. 4:11; Acts 20:19; Prov. 5:15-19). These would be desires for food, drink, sleep, or sex.

2. Neutral desires are wants, aspirations, or cravings that would not violate the prohibitions or decrees of God (Rom. 14:1-23). These would be the desires to go fishing, to be an engineer, to have one's own business, to play some professional sport, etc.

3. Noncompliant desires are sinful according to Scripture and should not be considered or acted upon (Rom. 13:13-14; 1 Pet. 4:1-5; Gal. 5:16-23). These would be desires such as killing, having someone else's wife or husband, having ultimate autonomy, seeking revenge, coveting, attending sinful parties, etc.

God does not want us to satisfy natural or neutral desires in a sinful manner or to satisfy any noncompliant desires (1 Pet. 1:14, 2:11; 1 John 2:15-17). For example, we should not satisfy natural desires in ways disobedient to God (e.g., gluttony, oversleeping out of laziness, sex outside of God's will). In addition, we are not to satisfy neutral desires in ways disobedient to God ((e.g., being dishonest on an application to get an engineering job, spending more than we can afford to have a nicer home, focusing so much on creating a business or invention that we neglect being a disciple or making disciples, or going fishing or playing video games so much that we neglect going to church or serving others). Finally, we are not to satisfy noncompliant desires at all (i.e., lust of the eyes, lust of the flesh, and the pride of life).

The material aspect of a person refers to the physical body that consists of all the physical features one sees externally and internally. These features enable humans to function on earth. For example, a person has physical parts such as brain, heart, arms, legs, hands, feet, and fingers. The physical body and the nonphysical part of a person are inseparably united while he is alive on earth (Gen. 2:7; 1 Cor. 15:35-38; Phil. 1:19-23).

The nonphysical and material aspects function somewhat like a car. Generally, when you drive a car, it goes in the direction you turn its steering wheel. The car carries out the will of the driver. (This illustration unfortunately breaks down in some situations!) Similarly the physical aspect of a person carries out what the nonphysical part of the person commands. Your body is the "vehicle" you drive while you are alive on earth.

We did not create ourselves, a truth suggesting that we were not designed to live according to our own ideas. It follows that we cannot really understand who we are or how we are to function, apart from connecting to our Creator. Therefore, to believe that a person can self-actualize, find himself, determine his destiny, or control the outcome of his life does not line up with the way he was created.

THE FALL OF HUMANITY

The Bible reveals that Adam and Eve committed the original sin in the Garden of Eden as they disobeyed God, eating the fruit that He commanded them not to eat (Gen. 3:1-13). Their sin resulted in negative consequences for their lives and also the lives of all humans. Let's explore some of the effects of Adam's and Eve's sin on their lives and on all their descendants—including us. The "Fall" is the term often used for this reality.

As a result of Adam's sin, all of humanity was placed in the position of sinner before God (Rom. 5:12-21, 3:10). In addition, Adam's sin led to all of humanity's being born with a sin nature, also known as inherited sin (Ps. 51:5; Jer. 17:9; Gen. 6:5; Matt. 15:15-20; Rom. 8:7; Rom. 7:7-24). Adam's sin led to every human's walking in individual sin before God and others (Rom. 3:10-18, 23; Eccl. 7:20; Rom. 8:5-8).

Furthermore, Adam's sin caused humanity to experience spiritual death: the separation of humans from the influence of God's power, presence, promises, indwelling, fellowship, and communication, and instead being under the control of the devil and his system of living (Eph. 2:1-5). Adam's sin also led to humanity's encountering physical death, as the spirit of each human becomes separated from the physical body when physical life ceases (Jas. 2:26). The ultimate consequence of Adam's sin on humanity is the experience of eternal death: separation from God after physical death into eternal punishment and damnation (Rev. 20:4-15; John 3:16-18).

The Fall's horrific result: Each human is influenced and controlled by sin in all aspects of his life. For example, because of Adam's sin, each person lost the ability to know himself accurately (Jer. 17:9). Sin has also led humans to worship self and creation above God (Rom. 1:18-32; 2 Tim. 3:1-5; Luke 12:13-21). Consequently, each person seeks to set himself up as an autonomous being, redefining good and evil according to his own standard (Ps. 14:1-3). Sin has caused each person to lose his ability to reason properly and weakened his ability to discern good and evil (Prov. 14:12). As a result, Adam's sin has crushed people's ability to judge the universe accurately, making it a god to worship instead of a responsibility to manage (Rom. 1:18-25). People have begun using other people and loving things, instead of loving people and using things (Rom. 1:18-25).

Some years ago a well-known ice cream company had to shut down because the ice cream became contaminated. No one knew where the contamination began or ended. The company leaders realized that their contaminated equipment had threatened the integrity and safety of every flavor of their ice cream. This is what sin has done to humanity. Sin did not just contaminate one generation, age, or ethnicity but all people groups and every person.

In summary, Adam's sin has permeated human nature and led to positional sin, conditional sin, and practical sin in the life of every person. Sin has led each person to believe that she can live in complete sufficiency and autonomy without living for and depending on God at any level. As sin has seduced each person to focus on herself, it has also pulled her away from the reality of her need for God and the reality that she was created to live for God. Where secular self-esteem leads people to focus on themselves, it demonstrates the influence and dominance of Adam's sin.

THE REDEMPTION OF HUMANITY

Although each person is a fallen creature and in need of deliverance from his positional sin, conditional sin, and practical sin, God provided very good news: another way through the gospel of Jesus Christ. This gospel can deliver a person from his sin condition and into a new and right relationship with God. Let's discuss the gospel, salvation, and the implications for humanity.

According to Romans 3:23, every human has failed to live up to the standards of God and to demonstrate His character. This is called sin. The punishment and payment for sin is that humans are separated from God in life and in relationship and at death will be placed in the eternal lake of fire to burn in hell for all eternity, apart from receiving the gift of eternal life in Jesus Christ (Rom. 6:23; Rev. 20:15). Jesus Christ, who is God and the Son of God the Father, came to earth, took on a human body, and lived a perfect life. He was crucified, buried, and resurrected in order to take the punishment and pay the penalty for the sins of humanity (1 Cor. 15:1-4).

A person can be delivered from his sin condition and restored to the relationship established with God before the Fall of Adam and Eve (2 Cor. 5:14-20). In order for this to happen, a person must put his trust in Jesus Christ, who sacrificed Himself to save those who trust Him from the condition and consequences of sin (John 3:16; Acts 3:19; John 17:3). When a person does this, he will be delivered from the penalty, the power, and eventually the presence of sin to a new and right relationship with God through His Son, Jesus Christ.

However, if a person refuses to do this, she will spend the rest of her life separated from God, living a life of sin, and spend eternity in hell as payment for her sin. These are the judgments for unbelief in Jesus Christ (John 3:18; Eph. 2:1-3, 5:5-6). On the other hand, if a person puts her trust in the Person and work of Jesus Christ, she will be placed in the family of God, identified as a child of God, and reconciled to a right relationship with God (John 1:12; 2 Cor. 5:17-18). A person must know God's Son, Jesus Christ, in order to be like Christ and useful to Christ (Phil. 3:8-11).

Several wonderful changes occur as a result of becoming a child of God and being reconciled to a right relationship with God the Father through His Son, Jesus Christ. A person will be given God the Holy Spirit to dwell within his nonphysical nature (Eph. 1:13-14). God the Holy Spirit then assures him that his salvation in Jesus Christ is secure and that all the promises coming with salvation will happen (Eph. 1:13-14). God the Holy Spirit will guide this person into the right direction in his relationship with God and empower him to obey God as he walks by God's power (Rom. 8:3-4, 14; Gal. 5:16).

If a person would like to receive this gift and be reconciled to a new and right relationship with God, he may confess with his mouth and believe in his heart that he is saved through the Person and work of Jesus Christ (Rom. 10:9-10). Here is an example of what a person could say to express sincere faith.

Father God, I understand that I am a sinner and need to be forgiven and delivered from my sin condition and have a restored relationship with You. I understand that You, Lord Jesus Christ, are God the Son, and that you took on a human body, and were crucified, buried, and resurrected to pay the penalty for my sin in order to deliver me from the penalty, the power, and soon the presence of sin into a new and right relationship with You and God the Father. I believe that this deliverance starts now and will continue in heaven. I understand, believe, and now entrust myself to You, Jesus Christ, as my Savior from sin, the Lord of my life, and my Reconciler into a new and right relationship with You and God the Father. Thank you, Jesus Christ, for saving me so that I may know You and God the Father. Thank you, God the Holy Spirit, as you now take residence in my soul and will guide me into this new and right relationship and empower me to obey. May You now lead me, oh God, to the church that will teach me how to live in this new life I have with You.

We can see that salvation is deliverance from the penalty, power, and soon the presence of sin through the death, burial, and resurrection of Jesus Christ into a right relationship with God the Father (John 1:12; Eph. 1:4-7, 2:8-10; 1 Cor. 15:1-4; 1 Pet. 1:18-19). Through salvation in Jesus Christ, people will gain spiritual life, which is the connection to the influence of God's power, presence, promises, indwelling, fellowship, and communication with Him (Eph. 2:1-22,

1:13-14). In addition, people will gain eternal life, a connection in relationship and fellowship with God forever (John 17:3). People also will be made useful and productive for God's agenda (Eph. 2:8-10; Rom. 7:4) and able to please God (Gal. 1:10; Phil. 3:1-21).

When I was young I enjoyed the TV show "The Six Million Dollar Man." The lead character portrayed an astronaut whose body was crushed in a terrible flight accident. However, scientists rebuilt him with bionics and made him essentially a "superman," stronger and faster than he was before.

In an even more complete way in body and nonphysical aspects, we have been broken by sin. But those of us who have put our faith in the Person and work of Jesus Christ have been supernaturally reborn and made better than we were before. We stand redeemed and revived in Christ Jesus our Lord!

As we saw in chapter 1, secular self-esteem concepts do not consider the message of the gospel and the gift of salvation as central components to a person's well-being, sense of identity, or ability to function at full capacity in his existence. Humans are considered the source of their own satisfaction and solution to their own problems. However, in a biblical framework of self, each person is seen as a sinner in need of salvation from God. The Bible asserts that we humans were created to live for Someone bigger than ourselves. It follows that each person must be delivered from himself instead of being self-actualized through the help of secular self-esteem.

GOD'S AGENDA FOR HUMANITY

Humans are not independent beings created to find their own destiny. Humanity was created with purpose. Secular self-esteem concepts portray humans as creating or finding their own purpose through the help of self-esteem. According to a biblical framework of self, humans surrender themselves to God and operate by the agenda

God has given them to accomplish (Rom. 12:1-8). The following list describes a general overview of humanity's purpose for existence.

First, humans were created to bring glory to God in all aspects of life (Isa. 43:7; Rom. 11:36; Col. 1:15-17; 1 Cor. 10:31; 2 Cor. 5:9,15; Matt. 5:14-16). To glorify God means to demonstrate the greatness of His character by functioning according to His design and will in all aspects of life, seeking to do everything in life with the intent of pleasing God (Eph. 5:7-17). Pleasing God would suggest doing what God has commanded by faith in the Person and promises of God (Rom. 12:1-2; Heb. 11:6).

Second, humans are to socialize with God for whom we were created. To socialize with God is to seek to know Him intimately through obedience and acquiring knowledge through the Word of God (John 17:3, 14:21). Humans must move beyond intellectual knowledge into a true experiential knowledge of God (Eph. 3:14-19; Heb. 11:6). This means coming to know God in practice and reality in a way others may only understand in theory.

Third, humans are to seek sanctification in Jesus Christ. That means maturing to reflect the character of Jesus Christ in all aspects of life (Eph. 4:11-32; Col. 3:1-25). This maturity should result in reflecting Jesus Christ in character, conduct, service, and relationships with others (Luke 6:40-46; John 13:33-35, 15:1-7). Humans were designed in God's image to function this way from the beginning of creation.

Fourth, humans are to build God-honoring churches that develop communities in which those who have trusted in Jesus Christ experience the love of God from and for one another (Heb. 10:24-25; 1 John 1:1-3; Rom. 12:8-13; John 13:33-35). Such churches seek to keep harmony among fellow Christians (Eph. 4:1-3; Rom. 12:18; 1 Pet. 3:8-12). They also maintain a bond of unity while encouraging one another, supporting one another, and showing kindness and compassion (Phil. 2:1-4; Col. 3:12-14).

Fifth, humans are to seek to serve God by serving others. To serve God means that a person makes himself useful to and pleases God by using the abilities and resources given to him by God to help others (Matt. 25:34-40; Eph. 2:10; Rom. 7:4, 12:1-8; 1 Pet. 4:10-11). For example, a person should strive to be an instrument of God by presenting the gospel of Jesus Christ, so that God may perhaps deliver sinners from their sin into a new and right relationship with Him that will last for eternity (2 Cor. 5:11-21; 1 Cor. 3:5-9). A person is also to help those who are already saved in Jesus Christ to grow to maturity in their character and faith in Him (Eph. 4:11-16; Col. 1:28-29). Consequently, a person is to bear burdens, meet needs, and speak the truth in love in hopes of salvation of the lost and sanctification of the saved (Gal. 6:1-3; Titus 3:14; Eph. 4:29).

Overall, a person is created to organize her life around following the directions and example of Jesus Christ in all aspects of life as prescribed in the Bible, resulting in being a sincere follower of Jesus Christ (Matt. 28:18-20; John 8:31-36). Thus, a person can live in a way pleasing to God and beneficial to herself (Prov. 3:5-8). Instead of self-actualization, this person will experience life transformation through the power of God (Col. 1:1-3:4).

Imagine being sent to run an errand for someone such as your boss. He gives you instructions on where to go and the list of supplies you need to bring back. You carefully follow his instructions, only to discover that you were given the wrong instructions, resulting in getting the wrong supplies. This happens to so many people. They are following the wrong instructions given by the wrong boss, because they are receiving their directions from the culture and the doctrine of demons. As a result, they try to build self-esteem instead of building a relationship with Jesus Christ.

God's agenda for humanity does not include a person's seeking to feel good about himself or "finding himself." It does not even focus on man's having self-confidence, believing in himself, or self-actualizing to be the best version of himself. The agenda for human-ity is to glorify and know God, to reflect the character of God, and to be useful to God in relationship to others, thereby leading to salva-tion and sanctification. We cannot depend on self, love self, or be consumed with self to accomplish this agenda. We must have a right relationship with God. This cannot be realized through the concepts of secular self-esteem.

SUMMARY

Humans have been created for the purpose of knowing God, reflect-ing the character of God, and being useful to God. Each person has been designed with material and nonphysical aspects so that he may function on earth as ordained and commanded by God. God has control over humans and the entire universe. People were never designed to function outside of the moral commands of God.

The idea that a person is at the center of his own existence, inher-ently good, and able to determine his destiny apart from any need of God directly contradicts the reality that each person is a sinner in need of a Savior and cannot determine his destiny apart from the Creator who has set an agenda for him. The theories that self-esteem is the key to a person's problems and solutions both personally and socially also deny the Creator God as the key to a person's problems and solutions. The idea that the well-being of a person is highly con-nected to his self-esteem does not line up with the facts presented above that his well-being is based upon his position and condition before God.

As we learn and understand these truths, we can evaluate the claims of secular self-esteem in light of a biblical perspective. The dif-ferences between the two perspectives come into clear focus. For Christians, this should raise concerns about adopting into our lives the concepts of secular self-esteem presented in chapter 1. The following chapter will merge what we have discussed thus far, demonstrating the contrast and incompatibility of a biblical framework of self with secular self-esteem theories of the twentieth- and twenty-first centuries, as propagated by many philosophers, psychologists, and Christian leaders.

Chapter 3

SECULAR IDEAS OF SELF-ESTEEM vs. A BIBLICAL VIEW OF SELF

Howdo *you* view *you*? If you haven't allowed the secular sea surrounding us to soak into your attitudes about yourself, you are an unusual Christian indeed. It's hard to swim against that current!

We can see that the various secular definitions of and approaches to self-esteem elevate humans as the ultimate beings and exclude God. They lead a person to pursue a life for self instead of living for God. Consequently, each person's overarching goal is to self-actualize through developing or maintaining self-esteem. The secular definitions and models of self-esteem assert that a human has the ability to be self-sufficient and cure himself of whatever bothers him through applying any of the various models of self-esteem. The Enlightenment period in eighteenth-century Europe promoted the belief in human self-empowerment and faith in human reason. The secular definitions and theories of self-esteem evaluated within this book promote the same: a belief in human self-empowerment and faith in human reason.

But here is what the Bible tells us: We should not allow the wisdom of the world to take us captive (Col. 2:8). Romans 3:23 affirms that all have sinned and fall short of God's glory. In addition, Jeremiah 17:9 reveals that man's heart is deceitful and sick. Psalm 58:3 highlights the idea that people are born wicked. Romans 3:10 states that no man is righteous according to God's standard. Thus each person's problem is essentially a sin condition, not a self-esteem need.

SECULAR THEORIES OF SELF-ESTEEM IN LIGHT OF A BIBLICAL FRAMEWORK OF SELF

The five central theories that the concept of self-esteem simplified—the ratio of achievement and expectation, positive and negative self-regard, inferiority complex, the impact of human relationships on one's view of self, and attachment theory—notably focus on a person's view of himself. However, these theories do not consider how each person was created to view himself or how the Fall of Adam and Eve into sin has impacted the way a person views himself. In addition, the Human Potential Movement promotes the idea that each person is the center of her existence, inherently good, and able to determine her destiny apart from any need of God. This movement thereby contradicts a biblical framework of self that recognizes the Fall of humanity into sin and humanity's need of God at all times. The influential California Task Force regarded self-esteem as the key to human problems and solutions both personally and socially, without considering the nature of sin or the redemption of humans from sin as matters of concern related to humanity's problems. Positive psychology also focuses on self-esteem as the underlying foundation to people's well-being and does not even consider sin, redemption, the nature of humanity, or humans as created in the image of God in relation to people's well-being.

I am definitely not considered a good cook. However, I sometimes try to cook a meal for my wife. When I don't include her in the project, I usually miss some essential ingredient that leaves the meal tasting not so great. My wife loves blueberry muffins, buttered and hot out of the oven. One night while she was sick, I heated up a left-over blueberry muffin and took it to her to eat. As soon as she saw it, she looked at me and (you guessed it) said, "Honey, can you get the butter, please?" I forgot the one central element that makes her muf-fin good. The muffin doesn't taste the same without it!

A friend told me about another type of problem we can have when cooking. From her backyard garden and trees, she harvested and froze some cherry tomatoes and small pitted plums. Deciding to make homemade spaghetti sauce, she grabbed the unlabeled bags of plums that looked just like little frozen tomatoes. Not realizing the mistake (she admitted the odd fragrance should have been a hint), she proudly served her family the sauce with pasta. After one bite they realized it was totally inedible. Even the dog refused it.

Just as the essential ingredients were missing or wrong ingredients were included in these meals, leading to cooking failures, so it is when people try to solve the issues of life without God. They leave out or try to replace the essential ingredients—central concepts like sin, salvation, or sanctification. No wonder we create a mess of every-thing without Him!

Key scholars such as William James, Robert White, Morris Rosen-berg, Stanley Coopersmith, Nathaniel Branden, Christopher J. Mruk, and Seymour Epstein (referenced in the Chapter 1 bibliogra-phy) developed foundational definitions of self-esteem that have been promoted and used by researchers. However, none of their def-initions or insights considered the impact of sin on a person's view of himself, which shows incompatibility with a biblical view of self. Most self-esteem theorists evaluate self-esteem's cause or effect, as well as the negative or positive impact of self-esteem on the well-being of humans, to determine how important self-esteem is to human existence. On the other hand, these theorists and theories do not discuss or present a relationship with God or lack thereof as an issue of vital importance to people's existence or well-being. They do not consider the nature of sin, salvation, sanctification, and eternal damnation (all crucial to a biblical framework of self) and how these would affect people's existence or well-being.

As a professor of biblical counseling, I assign many case studies to my students. One big challenge for these students is to avoid getting caught up in the details of the case, leading to human observations without a biblical interpretation and resulting in wrong conclusions and unbiblical solutions. For instance, one student became too focused on the background details in the case of a young woman who was very preoccupied with her mother's past behavior with multiple boyfriends. The student started making assumptions about the daughter's attitude toward her mother. The student then overlooked the present problem, which was the young woman's anger toward her mother's present boyfriend, and the biblical solution was therefore neglected.

When it comes to the issues of life, secular self-esteem theorists also have become consumed with the details of life and their own ideas, leading to human observations without a biblical interpretation and resulting in wrong conclusions about self-esteem and unbiblical solutions.

Secular self-esteem models tend to focus on one's self-confidence or self-rejection, as a significant aspect of research. According to these researchers, one's ability to excel in life is connected to his self-confidence or self-rejection. Yet what is considered insignificant or even lacking in their research is how an individual's rejection or acceptance of God and of God's understanding of humanity will impact one's ability to function or excel in a God-designed life. Consequently, secular self-esteem models contradict the idea that a person who puts confidence in himself is a fool (Prov. 28:26), thereby demonstrating incompatibility with a biblical framework of self.

I am 5'5" and a half (I appreciate the doctor giving me that half).

No matter how much I believe in myself, I will not on my own be able to dunk a basketball on an NBA regulation goal. I can visualize it, I can conceptualize, and I might even think positive thoughts about myself, but it will not give me the ability to dunk a basketball on my own. My life cannot revolve around confidence in my abilities but rather confidence in the abilities of Jesus Christ to empower me to do what He wants and not what I will. Believing in yourself does not give you power to do what you were not designed to do; it fools you into thinking you can do what you cannot. That is the deception of secular self-esteem.

In the secular self-esteem movement, researchers are oriented toward evaluating and thinking about self, but Scripture indicates that life is to be centered on the reality of God and His sovereignty (Eccl. 9:1, Jer. 10:23). In summary, humanistic psychology, through its definitions and models of self-esteem, contradicts God's view of humans, revealing an unbiblical view of self, a preoccupation with self, and a rejection of the reality of every person's sinful nature and need of God.

THE INCOMPATIBILITY OF TWENTIETH- AND TWENTY-FIRST-CENTURY SELF-ESTEEM CONCEPTS WITH A BIBLICAL FRAMEWORK OF SELF

The secular definitions and approaches to self-esteem attempt to redefine what it means to be human. A person is not seen as a sinner in need of a Savior. She is seen as a good person in need of adjustment, balance, and self-actualization. Humans become the center of all, leading to the worship of creation above the Creator. In fact, three central points about secular self-esteem contradict the biblical framework of self.

First, secular self-esteem definitions and models imply that each person is the central focus of his own existence. Determining whether a behavior is right or wrong depends on a person's lack of or need of self-esteem. How a person views himself in the context of his life is essential to his existence. Therefore, the main focus of each person is to improve himself or to become a better self. As a result, God is not the center of that person's life; each person is the center of his own life, leading to worship of self.

Second, the secular definitions and approaches to self-esteem suggest that a person has a need for worthiness and a right to esteem herself, instead of focusing on her unworthiness and need to esteem God. If Christians embraced this mindset, then the church would become a place where people serve themselves. In addition, members of the church would evaluate the church on how well the other members fed their "need for worthiness." Consequently, Jesus Christ would not be the center of worship. People would become the center of worship. A focus on worthiness can lead a person away from a focus on God.

Third, the secular definitions and approaches to self-esteem direct a person to focus on his own value instead of his depravity and need for redemption. The issue for a person should not be his value but the reality of what he has become with or apart from God. Consequently, a person must see himself in light of his need for reconciliation with God as opposed to his own value. Self-actualization and stability of personhood through pursuing or maintaining self-esteem cannot be a person's priority. Confession of sin, repentance of sin, and submission to the will of God must become the focus of humans.

A few years ago a TV show called "House" became popular. Dr. House specialized in finding the causes and treatments for the most difficult medical cases that no one else could solve. The show had a central theme. His assistants and others would cover every base to find the answers but ultimately would miss the simple but obvious issues causing the problem. By the end of each week's show, Dr. House would explain or demonstrate to them the solution. Secular self-esteem concepts comprise various details that seek to address man's problems. However, these concepts come up short because they miss the simple, obvious issues tied to sin, God, salvation, and sanctification.

Romans 1:18-32 reveals that God's wrath has come upon humans because they have chosen to reject God and set up their own ideas for life and existence. The text reveals that humans choose to worship the creation above the Creator. In essence, a person becomes a worshiper of herself and the creation around her. As a result, the preoccupation with self above the preoccupation with God has led to the self-deification we can see in the movement of self-esteem. Self-love, so the secular theorists say, then becomes the fuel for loving others. Consequently, focusing on self instead of focusing on God becomes the driving force for a person's ability to function and thrive in life.

Matthew 16:24 affirms the fact that if a person will pursue Jesus Christ, he must deny himself. In addition, 2 Timothy 3:1-2 states that difficult times will come because people will be lovers of themselves. Romans 8:5-6 reveals that a mind set on self leads a person to death, but a mind set on God leads a person to life and peace. Anything that promotes a life focused on self is a contradiction to the call of God for man. According to Dietrich Bonhoeffer, when a man is called to God, he is called to die to himself. Secular ideas of self-esteem tend to focus on building up self instead of following Jesus Christ.

Proverbs 3:5 tells people to trust in the Lord and not to lean on their own understanding. Proverbs 28:26 states that the person who trusts in his own heart is a fool. John 3:19 reveals that people love darkness instead of light. Consequently, people embrace the foolishness of their own ideas above the light of God. The secular approaches to self-esteem promote a trust in one's own knowledge and abilities, leading people away from their true need of forgiveness of sin and for salvation in Christ Jesus.

Imagine coming to me as your friendly neighborhood psychiatrist. You tell me about an inch-long nail stuck in the side of your head and the pain it causes you. After listening to your story, I share with you how we need to explore your view of yourself so you can begin to embrace yourself better. I then prescribe pain medication to help you feel better. In addition, I assign you to look in the mirror and hug yourself tightly, while repeating *I love myself, I love myself, I love myself.* Eventually, as the pain medication kicks in and you embrace yourself more, you may begin to feel better. However, the nail in the side of your head is the ultimate root issue that must be addressed. Concepts of secular self-esteem may help a person *feel* better, but they cannot lead a person to *become* better. These concepts do not address the central issues of a person's life: God, sin, salvation, and sanctification.

The basic need of humanity is not self-esteem. According to the authors of *Addicted to Recovery,* focusing on self-esteem reveals a heart of rebellion. A person's fixation on his own acceptance and worthiness is a refusal to accept his position and condition as a sinner before God. The pursuit of self-esteem promotes a high view of humans and a low view of God, consequently rejecting the reality of the sinfulness of humans and their need for God. The secular definition and approaches of self-esteem promote each person's faith in himself and rejection of his need for God.

A person's ability to do something or not to do something is not enabled or derailed by her self-esteem. Excusing or exalting behavior on the basis of self-esteem can lead people to believe that their abilities or lack thereof to handle life's situations depend on their high self-esteem or low self-esteem. This would place self-esteem in the category of a requirement for people to function and maintain a stable life condition. This line of reasoning does not match a biblical framework of self.

Galatian 6:7-8 states that a person has a choice to sow to the

Spirit or sow to the flesh. Romans 6:1-23 reveals that man is either a slave to sin or slave to God. Therefore, a person's actions are not determined by his level of self-esteem. His actions are determined by a heart motivated either by indwelling sin or by the Holy Spirit. Consequently, a person cannot blame his decisions on his level of self-esteem. According to Luke 6:43-45, a person's decisions are determined by the condition of his heart.

If the secular definitions and approaches to self-esteem are true, then we would assume that our ability to love is determined by our level of self-esteem. Therefore, we cannot love God or others without the empowerment of self-esteem. As a result, our ability to love is not empowered by the Holy Spirit but by our ability to obtain or maintain self-esteem. Consequently, we humans become the source of love for God and others. This idea directly contradicts a biblical framework of self.

The Apostle Paul writes in Galatians 5:22 that one slice of the fruit of the Holy Spirit is the ability to love. Galatians 5:16 commands us to walk by the Spirit. According to Scripture, a person's ability to love is not based on her level of self-esteem but on her level of submission to the Holy Spirit. Therefore, a person cannot love by looking to build her self-esteem but only by depending on the power of the Holy Spirit.

In 1 John 4:19 Scripture affirms that a person is able to love because he has been loved by God. John 13:34-35 explains that the model for love is not found within self, but in the character of Jesus Christ. In addition, 1 John 4:16 states that a person's ability to love reveals the evidence of God in his life, not the evidence that he has good self-esteem. According to Jim Owen, a person's prerequisite for love is not understanding and embracing self, but rather an appreciation for how much he has been loved by God. The ability to love is not based on a person's self-esteem but on his relationship with God or lack of it.

Imagine telling your spouse that because you do not feel good about yourself, you can't take out the trash or do anything that would demonstrate love because you just don't love yourself today. Or what if your spouse says to you, "I can't bring myself to provide you with some of the things you would like to receive from me because I just don't feel love worthy." Imagine your coworker explaining to you, "I can't finish this project because I don't feel good about myself." Being responsible is not contingent on a person's self-esteem.

Luke 9:23 informs each person that if he is going to follow Christ, he must deny himself, take up his cross, and follow Christ. This involves surrender of self to God and submission to the will of God in all things. It also requires preparing to suffer for the sake of God. We cannot live a life of self-fulfillment and self-focus and be a disciple of Christ. We cannot follow Christ and make self the center.

Romans 8:5-6 asserts that self-centered people have their minds on their sinful nature while God-centered people have their minds set on the things of God. This passage also reveals that God-centered thinking leads a person to the life and peace of God, whereas flesh-centered thinking leads him to death. According to Richard L. Mayhue (as quoted by John MacArthur and referenced in Chapter 2), a person will become what he or she intellectually and spiritually thinks. Therefore, he must think in a manner that keeps God at the center. This does not necessarily mean that he never thinks about self, but it does imply that a person will not be focused on self if he is to live a God-centered life.

According to Romans 12:3, a person must think according to what is right about himself and according to limitations given by God. In other words, his view of himself must be based upon standards set by God. Therefore, he will not think about himself in a way that does not align with what God says is true about him. Also, a person's view of himself will not be limited to his own opinion or the opinions of others. A person is not left to create a view of himself according to his own estimation but rather according to God's estimation. This can only happen if a person has faith in Jesus Christ. Apart from Jesus Christ, he is left to his own ideas about himself, as clearly seen in the secular ideas of self-esteem.

John 3:26-30 describes how John the Baptist had the proper assessment of his position before Jesus Christ. He embraced his role as the friend of the Bridegroom with humility and joy. He recognized his position was not to make himself big before the eyes of others but to make God big and himself small. John the Baptist was not focused on himself. John the Baptist was focused on Jesus Christ. Thinking about self in the proper context will not lead anyone to be focused on self but on God and God's mission.

Luke 18:9-14 recounts Jesus's story about a Pharisee and a tax collector, whose prayers revealed their views of themselves. The Pharisee had a prideful view of himself, resulting in his not being acceptable to God. The tax collector had a humble view of himself, resulting in his being acceptable to God. The text reveals that God will exalt people who are humble and will humble people who exalt themselves. A person's view of himself is not left to his own discovery and affirmation; he must view himself according to God's standard.

If a person does not walk in humility, she will not have the right view of herself and can expect the humbling from God. But if she walks in humility, she will have the right view of herself and can expect to be recognized by God. A person will not see herself rightly unless she sees herself within the light of God. Therefore, a person must be a Christian in order to have a right view of herself. In addition, she must be a Christian pursuing obedience to God in order to have a right view of herself.

So from a Christian perspective, a person who belongs to Christ is not to focus on self-esteem. A person who belongs to Christ is to focus on living rightly before the sight of God. A Christian is to understand who he is in his roles and responsibilities and who he is not, as well as how he is to operate in his roles and responsibilities. In addition, a Christian is to think about himself in such a way that leads him to repent of doing wrong and to walk in what is right. Consequently, a Christian is to focus on his actions and attitudes before others in ways to clearly show, through his roles and responsibilities, that he lives his life to promote the greatness of God.

Rather than being consumed with thoughts about himself (as unbelievers are about themselves), a Christian is to be consumed with what the will of God mandates for him to be and do. He is not to live to please self and focus on self. He is to live to please God—with self in the proper perspective—through the power that God provides. A Christian thus is to evaluate himself in order to understand who he is and who he is not, so that he may live in light of this truth to the glory of God.

When people apply for jobs, they read the job description to determine if they have what it takes to do the job assigned. They evaluate themselves in relation to the job description. God has given us a description of who we are, who we are to become, and our responsibilities. God has even given us the power to do what we are assigned to do according to whom He has made us. Our self-evaluation is then to help us understand who we are and who we are not, so that we may live in light of these truths to the glory of God.

SUMMARY

Ecclesiastes 9:1, Jeremiah 10:23, and Matthew 4:4 give us views of God as Sovereign Ruler, Sustainer, and Director of humanity in all aspects of existence. Therefore, a person does not have the ability to know himself accurately, guide himself properly, grow himself, or sustain himself apart from God. In an opposing view, the various models of self-esteem highlight each person as the center of his own existence, able to overcome the social ills of society and self-actualize with the help of self-esteem. For example, the developer of "person-centered counseling," Carl Rogers (referenced in Chapter 1), promoted the idea that individuals possess the answers within themselves to fix their own problems as they learn to love, respect, and accept themselves. Rogers stated that the answers to a person's problems are within himself through self-love, respect, and acceptance of self, but Jesus stated that a person cannot sustain himself apart from the Word of God.

If a person cannot determine the outcome of his existence, he cannot self-actualize as he chooses, which undermines the idea that self-esteem can help lead to his self-actualization. Thus a person's outcome cannot be determined by self-actualization but by the sovereign hand of God (Prov. 21:1). The concept of God's providence over mankind is antithetical to the self-esteem teachings we discussed earlier. Consequently, nothing in creation has the power to sustain or guide humanity into purpose and meaning except God. The secular approach leads a person to focus on self-dependence, while the other leads to dependence on God. Carl Rogers's and other similar approaches are thus incompatible with a biblical framework of self.

Chapter 4

A BIBLICAL COUNTERPOINT TO SELF-ESTEEM

Thinking back on your own life, can you recall some of the happy moments when you felt great—as though all was right in your world? Maybe someone you respected had complimented you on a difficult job well done, or you had just exchanged the first "I love you" with that special someone.

But those incredible feelings don't last forever, do they? Maybe you also remember other times, when everything seemed so awful that you would have to climb a tall ladder just to see out of the deep hole you had fallen in.

The word *self-esteem* brings up many concepts and ideas that we have discovered are antithetical to a biblical framework of self. The word is not found anywhere in the Bible and therefore should be used with caution when discussed in Christian circles. When I looked up the word in *Merriam-Webster's Collegiate Dictionary*, one of the definitions described it as a confidence and satisfaction in one's self, or self-respect. Does the Bible promote the idea that we should pursue confidence in self or be satisfied with ourselves or have self-respect? Actually, it does not. However, the Bible *does* present the idea that a person can feel good about himself or feel down on himself. The Bible even states the idea that one can have a confidence or fear and that these experiences and feelings are by-products of choices, not goals to pursue.

However, have you had times when you felt fear or confidence without being able to explain why? Where the culture has sought to use the term *self-esteem* to describe this phenomenon, let's consider the alternative concepts of conscience joy, conscience sorrow, confidence before God, and a lack of confidence before God. Before we discuss these concepts further, it would help to review our discussion on the conscience and then we will examine these corollary concepts.

THE CONSCIENCE

According to Romans 2:14-15, each person has a conscience that accuses him when he does wrong and excuses him when he does right in relation to what God defines as right and wrong. God challenged Cain with the idea that if he does what is right he will feel right and implied that if Cain did wrong he would feel bad (Gen. 4:1-7). Both of these passages reveal that each person has a conscience, the innate faculty in his nonphysical aspect that judges him as right or wrong in all he thinks, says, and does in relation to what God defines as right and wrong. This conscience makes him aware that he is responsible to God and accountable to God for the right he should do and the wrong he has done, resulting in a sense of pleasantness or unpleasantness in the heart (1 Sam. 24:1-15, 2 Sam. 24:10, 1 John 3:21). This pleasantness or unpleasantness in the heart can be defined as conscience joy and conscience sorrow.

Therefore, if a person functions in a way that is not right, he or she can expect to experience the unpleasantness in the soul that comes from the conscience: conscience sorrow (Rom. 13:1-5). However, if a person functions in a way that is right, he or she can expect to experience the pleasantness in the soul that comes from the conscience: conscience joy (2 Cor. 1:12). The state of unpleasantness and pleasantness in one's soul is not tied to one's feeling worthy or unworthy but to one's being guilty or clear of sin before the presence of God (Gen. 4:1-7, Rom. 2:14-15, 1 John 3:21).

Whether we feel worthy or not, if we do something that is wrong in the sight of God, we will experience unpleasantness in the soul (conscience sorrow). However, if we do something right in the sight of God, we will experience pleasantness in the soul (conscience joy). This is not based on our view of ourselves but on our choices to do right or wrong. This understanding does not line up with many secular theories we hear in relation to self-esteem.

CONSCIENCE JOY AND CONSCIENCE SORROW

The pleasantness and unpleasantness of the heart that we have described as conscience joy and conscience sorrow are not something we pursue but a by-product of right or wrong choices. The world has sought to define this phenomenon as high or low self-esteem. According to the secular humanistic perspective, this phenomenon is a pursuit to develop in or to develop out of. However, this phenomenon is not something to pursue, to work on, or to work out of, but is rather a by-product of our choices. Look at Genesis 4:3-7:

> So it came about in the course of time that Cain brought an offering to the LORD of the fruit of the ground. Abel on his part also brought of the firstlings of his flock and of their fat portions. And the LORD had regard for Abel and for his offering; but for Cain and for his offering He had no regard. So Cain became very angry and his countenance fell. Then the LORD said to Cain, "Why are you angry? And why has your countenance fallen? If you do well, will not your

countenance be lifted up? And if you do not do well, sin is crouching at the door; and its desire is for you, but you must master it."

Notice what God said to Cain: If you do right you will feel right. Cain's countenance or demeanor (his outward appearance revealing his feelings) was a by-product of his sinful anger toward God. Cain was not responding properly, and as a result he was experiencing conscience sorrow. His countenance and feelings were the direct result of a sinful choice, not the result of his situation or his environment. They were not the result of how he was treated, but rather the by-product of how he reacted! Cain was not just down; he was down on himself.

Consider Romans 2:14-15:

For when the Gentiles who do not have the Law do instinctively the things of the Law, these, not having the Law, are a law to themselves, in that they show the work of the Law written in their hearts, their conscience bearing witness and their thoughts alternately accusing or else defending them.

God made it clear that the conscience accuses us when we do wrong or defends us when we do right. This results in our experiencing conscience sorrow or conscience joy.

Consider 2 Samuel 24:10:

Now David's heart troubled him after he had numbered the people. So David said to the LORD, "I have sinned greatly in what I have done. But now, O LORD, please take away the iniquity of Your servant, for I have acted very foolishly."

The unpleasantness in David's soul was the experience of conscience sorrow as a result of committing sin. This feeling was not something created by David. This was a by-product of David's choosing to sin. David's conscience accused him, and he experienced the negative result.

Let's look at Romans 14:22-23:

The faith which you have, have as your own conviction before God. Happy is he who does not condemn himself in what he approves. But he who doubts is condemned if he eats, because his eating is not from faith; and whatever is not from faith is sin.

Where God has not given a prohibition or a decree in areas of life, God has given us the freedom to decide what we will and will not do before Him as our judge. Those decisions (in what we sometimes call "gray areas") are to be made in faith that God approves our decision to practice or not to practice in those areas. When we make those decisions in faith, knowing God is pleased with our decisions, we experience pleasantness in our souls (conscience joy). When we make those decisions in a lack of faith before God, thinking God would not be pleased, our hearts condemn us and we experience unpleasantness in our souls (conscience sorrow). Notice that the conscience joy and conscience sorrow are by-products of choices to walk in faith or sin, not objectives for us to pursue.

CONFIDENCE BEFORE GOD AND LACK OF CONFIDENCE BEFORE GOD

Consider these verses from 1 John and Proverbs:

> . . . *If our heart does not condemn us, we have confidence before God (1 John 3:21).*

> *The wicked flee when no one is pursuing. But the righteous are bold as a lion (Prov. 28:1).*

When a person does what is right according to Scripture, she has a sense of assurance that she is right before God. She has certainty that she is doing what pleases God. Her confidence is not in herself but in the fact that she is doing what God wants. This assurance is not based on a person's ability but on the conscience that affirms she is doing right before God. A person who does not have the fear of God's judgment, because she is not sinning, can be bold with confidence that she is pleasing God.

Consider 2 Corinthians 1:12:

> *For our proud confidence is this: the testimony of our conscience, that in holiness and godly sincerity, not in fleshly wisdom but in the grace of God, we have conducted ourselves in the world, and especially toward you.*

Note that their confidence is not in themselves but in the fact that they are walking rightly before God. This confidence is produced from the conscience, resulting from doing right in the sight of God. This confidence was a by-product of good choices and not a goal to achieve.

Confidence before God is different from having confidence in self. Whereas confidence in self leads us to focus on self, confidence before God leads us to focus on God. Confidence in self leads us to believe in self and trust in self, whereas confidence before God leads us to trust in God and draw near to God. The world encourages us to have confidence in self, but the Bible instructs us to trust in God and walk in obedience with God, which will produce a confidence before God. The world promotes assurance in ourselves; the Bible guides us into obedience to God. This will produce assurance that we are pleasing God and boldness to go before God's presence.

WHAT ABOUT A SEARED CONSCIENCE?

A seared conscience can happen when an unbeliever chooses to ignore his conscience in relation to conscience sorrow on a regular and consistent basis, resulting in suppressing the truth in unrighteousness and being given over to a depraved mind (Rom. 1:18-28). The person chooses to harden his heart to the unpleasant feelings associated with the sin choices he is making, which causes him to become callous (Eph. 4:17-19). He no longer experiences the unpleasant feelings associated with a guilty conscience. In other words, he is aware of his guilt and sin, but he no longer experiences pain from the guilt. His feelings of joy and sorrow become warped. He even affirms and encourages others to practice sin (Rom. 1:28-32).

Imagine having a clock that will tell time, but when you set the alarm, it doesn't make a sound. Unfortunately, you only learn of this problem by oversleeping and arriving late for an appointment! This clock is obviously broken, and you suffer the consequences. A seared conscience, like this broken clock, might appear to be OK. However, it will make a person aware that he is guilty of a sin but will no longer produce the conscience sorrow in him that should follow. This explains how people such as child abusers, serial killers, and others can commit horrible acts but apparently not have any conscience sorrow.

IMPLICATIONS

People or circumstances cannot produce within you any conscience sorrow, conscience joy, confidence before God, or a lack of confidence before God. You cannot produce in yourself some conscience joy or conscience sorrow or a confidence before God or lack of confidence before God. It is a by-product of your thoughts, words, and actions. If you are thinking, speaking, acting, or reacting in a sinful way toward God, people, or circumstances, you can expect conscience sorrow and a lack of confidence before God. If you are thinking, speaking, acting, or reacting in godly ways toward God, people, or circumstances, you can expect conscience joy and confidence before God.

When an unbeliever instinctively does what is right according to the work of the law written on his heart, he will experience conscience joy and confidence accordingly. He will feel good about himself and have a confidence in *himself,* rather than a confidence before God (Rom. 2:14-15, Phil. 3:1-6). Therefore, the confidence the unbeliever has is based on lining up with the work of the law written on his heart, not on God's righteousness produced by faith in Jesus Christ. Unbelievers can find themselves doing right and feeling good about themselves as a result, leading to a confidence in themselves and not a confidence in God. They are living for themselves and not for God, but they feel good about themselves because at some point in their decisions in that day or time, they did something right that resulted in the affirmation of their conscience (Rom. 2:14-15). Unless the Holy Spirit convicts and draws an unbeliever to accept Jesus Christ, he might instinctively do some things that are right from time to time, according to the work of the law written on his heart. He then trusts in himself that he is righteous apart from God (Phil. 3:1-6). He may even harden his heart in sin in the process (Rom. 1:28-32). However, he will experience conscience joy and confidence based on lining up with the work of the law written on his heart, resulting in drawing near to a false god (Rom. 1:21-23, 2:14-15; Phil. 3:1-6).

On the contrary, the believer will do right according to the work of the law written on his heart and the Word of God as guided by the Holy Spirit. As a result, he will experience conscience joy, as well as joy that comes from the Holy Spirit. This believer finds himself having confidence before God and moving toward God because he is driven by the Spirit of God. He is living for God and not himself, experiencing a joy that comes from doing what is right and from walking by the Holy Spirit (1 John 3:21-24, Gal. 5:16-22, Heb. 10:19-22). The universal reality for both believers and unbelievers is that when we do what is right, we will feel good about ourselves (conscience joy). When we do what is wrong, we will feel bad about ourselves (conscience sorrow). However, believers and unbelievers both experience conscience joy and conscience sorrow, but as we can see, each group goes in a different direction.

Your choices determine whether you will have conscience joy, conscience sorrow, confidence before God, or a lack of confidence before God. If a person says or does something to you, against you, or with you that is sinful, it does not mean that you will have conscience sorrow. To grieve is not a sin. To be disappointed is not a sin. That is merely feeling bad about the situation, not feeling bad about yourself. In fact, if you find that you have conscience sorrow because of what someone said or did to you, you have misdiagnosed the problem. Your sinful thoughts, words, or actions toward the person have led your conscience to convict you because your choices are sinful, which results in your feeling bad about yourself.

Think about the people around you. Do you believe they are contributing to your conscience joy or conscience sorrow? In reality, you are responding in a sinful way or a right way toward these people, which is producing conscience sorrow or conscience joy within you. When you do right you feel good about yourself, but when you do wrong you feel bad about yourself. Our environment, upbringing, and family do not cause our conscience joy or conscience sorrow; our choices do. Therefore, we must consider that others are not to blame for how we feel about ourselves. We must evaluate what we are thinking and doing in response to others.

SUMMARY

We have all, whether believer and unbeliever, been given a conscience by God. When we do right, our conscience encourages us, resulting in conscience joy. When we do wrong, our conscience convicts us, resulting in conscience sorrow. When we do what is right, we feel good about ourselves. But when we do what is wrong, we feel bad about ourselves. Your heart's condemning you or affirming you is the work of your conscience accusing you about some sin or encouraging you when you do what is right. The by-product of a right choice leads to conscience joy and confidence before God. But the by-product of a wrong choice brings conscience sorrow and a lack of confidence before God.

Conscience sorrow, conscience joy, confidence before God, or lack of confidence before God is tied to our reaction to God, people, and circumstances. Our loving or sinful attitudes and behaviors reflect our choices. When we walk in love toward God and others, we will experience conscience joy and confidence before God. When we walk in sin toward God and others, we will experience conscience sorrow and lack of confidence before God.

People or circumstances cannot produce conscience sorrow or

conscience joy within you. You cannot produce conscience joy or conscience sorrow in yourself or a confidence before God or lack of confidence before God. These feelings are by-products of your thoughts, words, and actions. If you are thinking, speaking, acting, or reacting in sinful ways toward God, people, or circumstances, you can expect conscience sorrow and a lack of confidence before God. If you are thinking, speaking, acting, or reacting in godly ways toward God, people, and circumstances, you can expect conscience joy and confidence before God.

Unbelievers do not have the Holy Spirit. They may from time to time adhere to and follow the work of the law written on their hearts or some standard in line with that work of the law, which will lead them to confidence in themselves and drawing near to a false god. Believers have the Holy Spirit. When submitting to the Holy Spirit, they then have confidence before God and draw near to Him. Believers and unbelievers both experience conscience joy and conscience sorrow, but each group follows a different path. Where the secular world speaks of self-esteem, we replace that concept with the biblical perspective of conscience joy and conscience sorrow. Whereas the world promotes self-esteem as something to pursue, biblically we recognize it as a by-product of choices and more appropriately describe it as conscience joy and conscience sorrow. Instead of being part of the trinity of self-worship, it becomes part of the triangle of self-evaluation.

Chapter 5

A BIBLICAL PERSPECTIVE
ON SELF-IMAGE

M IRROR, MIRROR ON THE WALL! Who's the fairest of them all?" Do you remember that iconic quote?

It seems that no matter where or who we are, we humans are concerned with who we are and how we look to others. Think of how many people make their living from their self-image. People such as movie or TV stars, musicians, politicians, business-men, and social-media personalities (some of them "famous for being famous") are concerned and even consumed with what people think of them. But what exactly is self-image, and how does the Bible speak to this?

Merriam-Webster's dictionary describes self-image as one's per-ception of one's self or one's role. This has to do with who we believe we are and who we believe we are not. It also reflects what we believe our roles are in life. Do you or I get to determine who we are and what our roles are in life? Has God determined this already?

Secular humanistic understanding of self-image could lead us to believe that we have the option to define or redefine who we are according to what we believe. However, when God created us, He had a specific design and order for us to operate in as man and woman (Gen. 1:26-30). From the very beginning, the first man and woman rejected that design and order, deciding to follow their own

---

understanding of life and creation (Gen. 3:1-10). As a result, self-image has become an amalgamation of ideas that keep individuals focused on defining and redefining themselves as they see fit.

From a biblical perspective, self-image is not something defined or redefined by each person's ideas about himself. Self-image is pre-scribed by what God has said to be true about each person. There-fore, he must look to God to understand who he is, who he is not, and what he is to become. If he does not have the view of himself that aligns with what God says is true about him, he has a false view of himself and thinks more highly of himself that he ought to think (Rom. 12:3).

In this chapter we will explore a biblical perspective on self-image as opposed to a secular humanistic idea of self-image. In order to understand self-image through a biblical perspective, we must first look at the biblical concepts of pride and humility.

PRIDE AND HUMILITY

What a person believes about himself is tied to an accurate or inac-curate view of himself. An accurate or inaccurate view of self is con-nected to the biblical concepts of pride and humility. Pride can be defined as a mind that is set on self with a lack of submission to the will of God. A prideful person upholds his own standard for think-ing, speaking, and behaving above God's standard. A prideful person has a view of himself based on his own opinions and ideas, apart from the truth of God's Word.

Let's consider these passages:

Psalm 10:3-4: For the wicked boasts of his heart's desire, and the greedy man curses and spurns the LORD. The wicked, in the haughtiness of his countenance, does not seek Him. All his thoughts are, "There is no God."

Romans 8:5-7: For those who are according to the flesh set their minds on the things of the flesh, but those who are according to the Spirit, the things of the Spirit. For the mind set on the flesh is death, but the mind set on the Spirit is life and peace, because the mind set on the flesh is hostile toward God; for it does not subject itself to the law of God, for it is not even able to do so, and those who are in the flesh cannot please God.

Acts 12:21-23: On an appointed day Herod, having put on his royal apparel, took his seat on the rostrum and began delivering an address to them. The people kept crying out, "The voice of a god and not of a man!" And immediately an angel of the Lord struck him because he did not give God the glory, and he was eaten by worms and died.

The word *pride* is not stated in any of these passages, but the concept is implied throughout. Each passage reveals a mind that is set on self with a lack of submission to God's will. The subject of each passage views himself by focusing on self or the opinions of others. This is the epitome of pride.

If a person builds her self-image on the opinions of others, the culture, and personal opinions, she will develop an inaccurate view of herself that will be a result of pride. It will lead the person to have an inaccurate assessment of herself before God and to trust in earthly, natural, demonic wisdom. Imagine if I were to convince myself that I am President of the United States, and I expected you to treat me as such. That would be delusional, wouldn't it! So it is when Christians seek to evaluate who they are and who they are not by their own opinions or the opinions of the culture.

Let's look at these passages:

Daniel 4:28-32: "All this happened to Nebuchadnezzar the king. Twelve months later he was walking on the roof of the royal palace of Babylon. The king reflected and said, 'Is this not Babylon the great, which I myself built as a royal residence by the might of my power and for the glory of my majesty?' While the word was in the king's mouth, a voice came from heaven saying, 'King Nebuchadnezzar, to you it is declared: sovereignty has been removed from you, and you will be driven away from mankind, and your dwelling place will be with the beasts of the field. You will be given grass to eat like cattle, and seven periods of time will pass over you until you recognize that the Most High is ruler over the realm of mankind and bestows it on whomever He wishes.'"

Luke 18:9-14: And He also told this parable to some people who trusted in themselves that they were righteous, and viewed others with contempt: "Two men went up into the temple to pray, one a Pharisee and the other a tax collector. The Pharisee stood and was praying this to himself: 'God, I thank You that I am not like other people: swindlers, unjust, adulterers, or even like this tax collector. I fast twice a week; I pay tithes of all that I get.' But the tax collector, standing some distance away, was even unwilling to lift up his eyes to heaven, but was beating his breast, saying, 'God, be merciful to me, the sinner!' I tell you, this man went to his house justified rather than the other; for everyone who exalts himself will be humbled, but he who humbles himself will be exalted."

Pride can lead us to set our minds on ourselves, which results in an inaccurate view of ourselves and self-destruction. God does not favor those who evaluate themselves according to their own standards or the opinions of others.

An accurate or inaccurate view of self is connected to the biblical concepts of pride and humility. Humility is defined as a mind that is set on Jesus Christ with submission to the will of God. Humility means embracing a view of self according to the standards of God and not the opinions of self or others. A humble person adjusts his standards to align with the will of God. Therefore, he understands who God says he is and operates according to that insight from God, resulting in obeying God and submitting to His will for life.

The following passages help explain these truths:

John 3:25-30: Therefore there arose a discussion on the part of John's disciples with a Jew about purification. And they came to John and said to him, "Rabbi, He who was with you beyond the Jordan, to whom you have testified, behold, He is baptizing and all are coming to Him." John answered and said, "A man can receive nothing unless it has been given him from heaven. You yourselves are my witnesses that I said, 'I am not the Christ,' but, 'I have been sent ahead of Him.' He who has the bride is the bridegroom, but the friend of the bridegroom, who stands and hears him, rejoices greatly because of the bridegroom's voice. So this joy of mine has been made full. He must increase, but I must decrease."

1 Corinthians 4:1-4: Let a man regard us in this manner, as servants of Christ and stewards of the mysteries of God. In this case, moreover, it is required of stewards that one be found trustworthy. But to me it is a very small thing that I may be examined by you, or by any human court; in fact, I do not even examine myself. For I am conscious of nothing

*against myself, yet I am not by this acquitted; but the one
who examines me is the Lord.*

In both passages, the men understood who they were and who
they were not according to what God established as the definitive
view of themselves. They aligned themselves to function according to
what God established. The word *humility* was not stated, but the
concept of humility was demonstrated in both of these passages.

If a person builds his self-image on what God says is true about
him according to Scripture, he will develop an accurate self-image.
This person ultimately will trust in Jesus Christ to explain who he is
and who he is not, therefore living by the wisdom of God.

When I am at the doctor's office and waiting for the receptionist
to call my name to go back to see the doctor, I am not tempted to get
up and go to the back when she calls someone else's name. I know
that the person she is calling is not me. And the more we adjust ourselves to embrace who God says we are and are not, the more we will
operate in humility and have an accurate self-image.

Let's consider these passages:

*Peter 4:14-16: If you are reviled for the name of Christ, you
are blessed, because the Spirit of glory and of God rests on
you. Make sure that none of you suffers as a murderer, or
thief, or evildoer, or troublesome meddler; but if anyone
suffers as a Christian, he is not to be ashamed, but is to
glorify God in this name.*

*2 Corinthians 5:17-18: Therefore if anyone is in Christ, he is
a new creature; the old things passed away; behold, new
things have come. Now all these things are from God, who
reconciled us to Himself through Christ and gave us the
ministry of reconciliation.*

If a Christian is walking in humility, he will understand who he is and who he is not and function according to God's standards. When walking in humility, his view of himself is guided and guarded by his relationship with Jesus Christ. Walking in humility leads to suffering for and serving the cause of Jesus Christ, as well as functioning as a new creature in Christ.

Remember Webster's definition of self-image as one's perception of one's self or one's role? In and of itself the definition does not contradict a biblical world-view. The issue is by what method a person comes to see himself. Does he embrace the standards of God to define who he is and who he is not? Or does he embrace his own ideals, or that of the culture and others, which ultimately is the doctrine of the secular culture and the preoccupations of the flesh. A person's self-image is not high or low but right or wrong. Self-image ultimately is an issue of pride and humility. If a person is walking in pride, he will have the wrong self-image. If he is walking in humility, he will have the right self-image.

SELF-IMAGE FROM A BIBLICAL PERSPECTIVE

Notice that self-image comes from a different perspective than conscience joy and conscience sorrow. Where conscience joy and conscience sorrow focus on how you feel about yourself as a result of choices you have made, the concept of self-image focuses on what you believe is true about yourself in relation to God, people, and situations. This gets into your perspective of who you believe you are and who you believe you are not.

Consider Romans 12:3:

For through the grace given to me I say to everyone among you not to think more highly of himself than he ought to think; but to think so as to have sound judgment, as God has allotted to each a measure of faith.

Conscience joy and conscience sorrow are not something you pursue but rather a by-product of your choices. However, self-image is something you develop according to the truth of God's Word. To have sound judgment about yourself is to think correctly about yourself according to the standards of God. It is to see yourself as God sees you, not according to your own or others' opinions.

You must learn what God says is true about you in order to have right thinking about yourself. Sometimes people's assessment of you is true, but sometimes it is an opinion. Their view of you should always be filtered through what God says is true about you. As my professor Stuart Scott once taught us in class, when someone gives their assessment of you, you should ask yourself two questions. First, is it true? And second, is it something I need to change?

If it is true and something you need to change, then through the power of God and the support of others, change it. (Of course, we know that sometimes change is a process and not instantaneous; the important thing is to move in the right direction.) But if it is not something that needs to be changed, then approach others about their perception or preference for you by saying that you will give some consideration as to how you may serve them in the matter without changing who you are. It seems the situation is more about what they want from you than who you are.

Who you are and who you are not is based on what God says, not what others think of you. If you do not have an understanding of what God says about you, then you will care too much about what others think of you rather than caring a lot about others. Herein lies the problem in many relationships. The self-image of one is determined by the opinions of the other instead of by the truth of God's Word.

DEVELOPING A BIBLICAL SELF-IMAGE

In order to develop a biblical self-image, we must look at areas of our lives where we lack submission to God and then begin to do what is necessary in those areas in order to walk by God's will. For example, we could evaluate various concepts of self that we believe and look at what the Bible says about those areas. As we compare what the Bible says and what we believe to be true about ourselves, we can replace inappropriate thinking with the proper thinking. This can help us take captive our inner thoughts that have risen up against the knowledge and character of God (2 Cor. 10:5). A proper view of self requires guidance from the Word of God so that we can see the various categories of sinner, saint, believer, unbeliever, fool, wise person, etc., and discover how they apply to ourselves. A disciplined study of these particulars can lead us into understanding where we are and need to be in functioning according to God's ordained plan.

Our identity does not depend upon what we do but what Jesus Christ has done. Therefore, as Christians we can embrace who we are in Christ, knowing we were made that way by God. We must be guided into understanding that all we are has everything to do with all that Christ has done (2 Cor. 5:17). Then we realize that our doing should be the direct result of our being—and not the other way around.

Therefore, as Ken Boa explained, only when a Christian defines himself through the truth of God's Word will he discover his deepest identity. Boa explained that Christians tend to allow the opinions of others instead of the truth of God to define them. As we are restructuring our thinking, we can determine where we have allowed the dictates of others to define who we are. Then we can identify what God says in comparison and replace the opinion with the truth. Only then can we be sure not to allow other people's opinions to dictate our identity.

As a Christian develops in spiritual maturity, he must focus on the goal of a proper view of self. According to Randy Leedy, all Christians are destined to be conformed into the image of Jesus Christ. Therefore, a proper view of self has to be tied to a proper view of the character of Christ. Leedy describes conforming into the image of Jesus Christ as a process of spiritual growth. All of the various avenues we have discussed to nurture a proper view of self must have the ultimate goal of Christians' seeing themselves through Jesus Christ's character. If not, their efforts are merely exercises in self-preoccupation instead of Christ-like transformation.

Becoming like Christ in our identity would suggest that we must learn and grow in the character of Christ. According to Randy Jaeggli, the foundation of experience in the Christian life depends on how much or how little we learn about and embrace the character of God.

Consequently, the more or less we learn about God's character will determine how well we develop in a biblical view of self. As God exposes and reveals who He is, we must come to learn who we are in connection to God (Isa. 6:5). Therefore, developing a proper view of self will not happen without learning about and embracing the proper view of God.

A Christian's relationship with God is possible through embracing the knowledge He reveals and the Holy Spirit's application of that knowledge to the person's life. As we incorporate the knowledge, we can cultivate a proper view of ourselves. A relationship with God requires death to self. In developing a proper view of self, we must walk in humility so that we can die to who we have been in order to become new in Jesus Christ. According to Andrew Murray, humility is the path to death of self, which leads to the process of perfecting the individual into the character of Christ. While developing a proper view of self, we can identify the things about self that are not like Christ and begin the hard work of repenting of those things. Murray asserts that the proof we have given ourselves to Christ is when we die to self. This again shows the importance of developing a proper view of self in order to have a life of obedience to Christ.

According to Dietrich Bonhoeffer (as referenced in Chapter 3), Christ became like man so that man can become like Him. Therefore, the proper of view of self will be seen in the model that Jesus provided for people to follow. The study of Scripture will reveal the various attitudes and behaviors of Jesus. As we study Jesus's reactions to various people and circumstances, we can learn how to think, speak, and act. We can learn who we are to be by looking to the model provided by Jesus Christ and, through fellowship with Christ, increasingly become like Him.

A proper view of self involves understanding that we have been designed to serve (Rom. 12:3-7). Therefore, it is important that we identify and use our spiritual gifts appropriately (1 Pet. 4:10-11). According to Don and Katie Fortune (as referenced in Chapter 2), we can only use our spiritual gifts at their fullest when we are dedicated to God. A proper view of self can lead us to see ourselves as bondservants who are to present our bodies as a living and holy sacrifice to God (Rom. 12:1).

According to Jim Berg (as referenced in Chapter 2), a Christian is to strive to develop in displaying the excellencies of God. In other words, we are to function according to the purpose for which we were created. Berg says that we are to become like Christ and to display that character to all. Developing a biblical view of self can lead Christians in understanding who we are, in order to function according to the purpose for which God created them. A biblical view of self can lead us into displaying knowledge, self-control, endurance, brotherly kindness, and love, thereby demonstrating the character of Jesus Christ (2 Pet. 1:1-9).

In summary, in order to have a biblical self-image we should see ourselves as God sees us and embrace this reality.

1. We should see ourselves as created in the image God, knowing we were

   • Created to reflect God's character (Gen. 1:26-31)

   • Created to be relational (Gen. 2:18)

   • Created to be worshippers of God (John 4:23-24)

   • Designed with intellect (Prov. 23:7)

   • Designed with a will (Eccl. 2:4-8)

   • Designed with emotions (Acts 20:36-38)

2. We should view ourselves according to our biological design, considering that

   • If we were created male, we must view ourselves according to our male distinctions and functions (1 Cor. 11:1-12)

   • If we were created female, we must view ourselves according to our female distinctions and functions (1 Cor. 11:1-12)

3. We should view ourselves as fallen image bearers of God, considering that after the Fall of Adam we have become

   • Wicked by nature (Gen. 6:5)

   • Wicked in thoughts, words, actions (Matt.15:15-20)

   • A worshipper of the creation instead of the creator (Rom. 1:18-32)

   • A pursuer of sin and not a pursuer of God (Rom. 3:10-18)

- An enemy of God and in need of salvation (Rom. 8:7-8)

- Useless, sinful, unworthy, helpless, totally undeserving of anything (Rom. 3:10-18)

4. We should view ourselves according to our position in Christ, knowing that when in Christ, we are

- Forgiven of our sin against God (1 John 2:1-2)

- Greatly loved by God (John 3:16, Rom. 5:8)

- Placed in the family of God (Eph. 2:11-19)

- Made alive from within to connect with God (Eph. 2:1-10)

- Given the Holy Spirit to empower us to live as God desires (Rom. 8:12-17)

- Set apart to God and made useful and pleasing to God through the power of the Holy Spirit working in us (Eph. 2:8-10)

5. We should view ourselves according to the biblical roles we have been given, such as

- Husband/Wife (Eph. 5:18-33, Col. 3:18-19, 1 Pet. 3:1-12)

- Son/Daughter (Eph. 6:1-2, Col. 3:20)

- Parent (Eph. 6:4, Col. 3:21, Deut. 6:6-9, Prov. 22:6)

- Friend (Prov. 27:5-6; 17:17; 27:9; 18:24)

- Leader (1 Tim. 4:16, Heb. 13:7, 17; 1 Pet. 5:5, 1 Tim. 5:17-22, Luke 6:40)

- Employer/Employee (Eph. 6:5-9, 1 Pet. 2:18-29)

6. We should view ourselves according to our spiritual giftedness, realizing that

- We must see ourselves as servants with gifts to benefit the body (1 Pet. 4:10-11)

- We must know what our gifts are (1 Cor. 12:1-11)

- We must use our gifts accordingly (Rom. 12:3-8)

SUMMARY

A Christian is united with Jesus Christ (Rom. 6:1-23). That union provides a Christian with grace to overcome sin and live victoriously for Jesus. Consequently, every Christian has the ability through the power of God to put off the improper view of himself that leads to a life of sin. Moreover, every Christian has the ability through the power of God to put on a proper view of himself so that he may live a life of victory for Jesus.

As a Christian develops a proper view of self, he will come to terms with the reality that in Christ he is different than he used to be. In addition, he is now what he never was. According to Scripture, this person has been justified in Christ (Rom. 5:1). He has also been made a new creature (2 Cor. 5:17). Therefore, Christians are encouraged to live according to who they are in Christ instead of what they were in Adam (Col. 3:1-17).

As a result, Christians cannot embrace the twentieth- and twenty-first-century concepts of self-esteem promulgated by philosophers, psychologists, and Christian leaders. These concepts are incompatible with a biblical framework of self. Whereas the world promotes self-image as being high or low, biblically we recognize it as being accurate or inaccurate and as promoting pride or humility. Instead of being part of the trinity of self-worship, self-image can become part of the triangle of self-evaluation.

Chapter 6

A BIBLICAL UNDERSTANDING
OF SELF-LOVE

W<small>E'VE ALL HEARD</small> many clichés about loving ourselves. "You can't love anyone else until you learn to love yourself" is often said with a nod of certainty, as though everyone knows it's true. The concept that loving others requires me to love myself first does seem to contradict Jesus's assertion that the two greatest commandments are to love God and love others (Matt. 22:36-39). In fact, the Bible states that there are two great commandments and not three. From Genesis in the Old Testament through Revelation in the New, God has never asked us to love ourselves. Love for self is in an implied reality. The dictionary defines self-love as an appreciation of one's own worth, proper regard and attention to one's own happiness or well-being, and even an inflated love for or pride in oneself. What does the Bible say about self-love?

In *The Heart of Man and Mental Disorders* by Rich Thomson (as referenced in chapter 2), the author gives three categories of self-love. He describes self-love as selfish self-love, self-preserving self-love, and soul-loving self-love. Following are an explanation of each category and the implications for our lives.

SELF-ESTEEM, SELF-IMAGE, SELF-LOVE

SELFISH SELF-LOVE

Selfish self-love can be defined as making self the priority for life or making self the central interest of existence. Let's consider 2 Timothy 3:1-4:

> But realize this, that in the last days difficult times will come. For men will be lovers of self, lovers of money, boastful, arrogant, revilers, disobedient to parents, ungrateful, unholy, unloving, irreconcilable, malicious gossips, without self-control, brutal, haters of good, treacherous, reckless, conceited, lovers of pleasure rather than lovers of God.

Preoccupation with self breeds selfishness, conflict with others, and every evil thing. Let's look at James 3:13–4:3:

> Who among you is wise and understanding? Let him show by his good behavior his deeds in the gentleness of wisdom. But if you have bitter jealousy and selfish ambition in your heart, do not be arrogant and so lie against the truth. This wisdom is not that which comes down from above, but is earthly, natural, demonic. For where jealousy and selfish ambition exist, there is disorder and every evil thing. But the wisdom from above is first pure, then peaceable, gentle, reasonable, full of mercy and good fruits, unwavering, without hypocrisy. And the seed whose fruit is righteousness is sown in peace by those who make peace. What is the source of quarrels and conflicts among you? Is not the source your pleasures that wage war in your members? You lust and do not have; so you commit murder. You are

envious and cannot obtain; so you fight and quarrel. You do not have because you do not ask. You ask and do not receive, because you ask with wrong motives, so that you may spend it on your pleasures.

Notice that selfish self-love keeps us in a dangerous position of believing that life revolves around ourselves. Where there is selfish self-love, we will find self-indulgence, a sense of entitlement, hedonism, and a preoccupation with autonomy.

There is no place for selfish self-love in the life of a Christian. Therefore, the idea that we must learn to love ourselves before we can love God and others is not true. Selfish self-love is a contradiction to living for God, as this passage of 2 Corinthians 5:14-15 explains:

For the love of Christ controls us, having concluded this, that one died for all therefore all died; and He died for all, so that they who live might no longer live for themselves, but for Him who died and rose again on their behalf.

Many times people have come into my office describing how hard they have it, serving someone but receiving nothing in return. They have complained of lack of appreciation, as well as lack of concern or effort by the person who is the object of their affection. In reply, I asked them a simple questions that at first seemed easy but eventually became difficult and revealing. "For whom were you doing all that you were doing? Was it for the glory of God or your own benefit?" In those cases selfish self-love often paraded as love for God and others. Where there is selfish self-love, we find a need for repentance. We cannot be consumed with self and live for God at the same time.

SELF-PRESERVING SELF-LOVE

Self-preserving self-love can be defined as our natural tendency to take care of ourselves and preserve our material bodies. Consider Ephesians 5:28-29:

So husbands ought also to love their own wives as their own bodies. He who loves his own wife loves himself; for no one ever hated his own flesh, but nourishes and cherishes it, just as Christ also does the church.

The concept here is that everyone naturally takes care of him- or herself by instinct. When you are hungry you feed yourself. When you are in pain you seek relief. When you are thirsty you find something to drink. If you are sleepy you go to sleep. These are natural, normal things we do to look after ourselves. We do these things for ourselves without giving them a second thought. Since a husband has become one flesh with his wife, he is to treat her the way he treats himself. As he has the natural instinct to look after himself, he should have that same instinct to care for his wife. The text calls this natural instinct of looking after ourselves in this manner an act of self-love.

Self-preserving self-love is not sinful! It is a normal part of your day-to-day activity. It is not wrong to feed yourself, take a bath, rest when you're tired, brush your teeth, or take medicine when you need relief or healing that can come from that medicine. It does not prohibit you from loving God and loving others. However, if all you do is feed yourself, take a bath, etc., and do not consider the needs or interests of others, then you are no longer operating in self-preserving self-love. You are now operating in selfish self-love. This passage in 1 John 3:16-19 cuts to the heart of the matter:

*We know love by this, that He laid down His life for us; and
we ought to lay down our lives for the brethren. But
whoever has the world's goods and sees his brother in need
and closes his heart against him, how does the love of God
abide in him? Little children, let us not love with word or
with tongue, but in deed and truth. We will know by this
that we are of the truth, and will assure our heart before
Him.*

Having the world's goods to use for ourselves is not a problem.
Not sharing the world's goods we have with other Christian brothers
and sisters who are in need is a problem. Love uses what God has
allowed us to have for self and for others. Let's consider 1 Timothy
6:17-19:

*Instruct those who are rich in this present world not to be
conceited or to fix their hope on the uncertainty of riches,
but on God, who richly supplies us with all things to enjoy.
Instruct them to do good, or to be rich in good works, to be
generous and ready to share, storing up for themselves the
treasure of a good foundation for the future, so that they
may take hold of that which is life indeed.*

Imagine you are at the gas station and, as you are about to take your
last $20 to put some gas in your car, a church member from your
same small group drives up. After greeting you, he asks if he can bor-
row some money to help with some gas for his car. What do you do?
Self-preserving self-love would encourage you to take a portion of the
$20 and give it to your brother, while still putting some gas in your
own car. Selfish self-love would say, "Sorry, buddy. I'm all out of cash,
but I'll pray for you."

One can operate in self-preserving self-love and still love God and love others. When Jesus called us to deny ourselves, take up our cross, and follow Him, He did not mean we should not look after ourselves (self-preserving self-love) by no longer feeding ourselves or taking a bath or getting clothes for ourselves, etc. He meant we are not to be consumed with ourselves, considering no one but ourselves (selfish self-love), but rather we should live our lives for the glory of God.

SOUL-LOVING SELF-LOVE

Soul-loving self-love can be defined as a person's effort to get wisdom and understanding so that he may live righteously. As Proverbs 19:8 asserts, "He who gets wisdom loves his own soul; he who keeps understanding will find good."

Soul-loving self-love is essentially the attitudes and actions of a person who understands the importance of having the wisdom of God to live a life pleasing to God. People who attend to their souls in this manner will find that their quality of life is one of productivity and stability. This truth is described in Psalm 1:1-3:

> How blessed is the man who does not walk in the counsel of the wicked, Nor stand in the path of sinners, Nor sit in the seat of scoffers! But his delight is in the law of the LORD, And in His law he meditates day and night. He will be like a tree firmly planted by streams of water, Which yields its fruit in its season And its leaf does not wither: and in whatever he does, he prospers.

Notice that soul-loving self-love leads a person to attend to himself but not to be consumed with himself. He feeds his mind with truth so that he may live a life discerning and living out the truth. Romans 12:2 explains it clearly: "And do not be conformed to this world, but be transformed by the renewing of your mind, so that you may prove what the will of God is, that which is good and acceptable and perfect." This person may pray for wisdom (James 1:5), seek wise counsel from others (Prov. 19:20), or be guided into wisdom by the indwelling Holy Spirit as He makes the Word of God plain (1 Cor. 2:6-13).

A Christian cannot know, understand, and live out the will of God without feeding her soul on God's Word. Then developing in wisdom from that Word leads to a life of discernment and productivity according to God's will. Therefore, soul-loving self-love is not a self-centered, self-absorbed way of living. Such a Christian seeks to know and live within the guardrails and guidelines of God's will and ways. As 2 Timothy 2:15 says, "Be diligent to present yourself approved to God as a workman who does not need to be ashamed, accurately handling the word of truth." In order to present the Word for the sake of leading others to have lives pleasing to God, we need to feed on the Word of God to understand and live accurately and winsomely.

What if someone came up to you and asked, "How do you spend your time?" And suppose you responded by saying, "I spend a lot of my time studying and meditating on God's Word." Then they surprised you by replying, "That is just selfish! Why aren't you out doing something productive for the Lord?" Doesn't that sound strange to you? Soul-loving self-love isn't selfish at all. It is the pursuit of godly wisdom in order to live a godly life.

IMPLICATIONS

In any relationship, the only self-love that can create problems is selfish self-love. If we grow increasingly preoccupied with our own world and how it is impacted by everything around us, we can begin to live as if the only person we need to answer to or consider is ourselves. This leads to conflict in relationships and a lot of disorder, because we are leaning on our own understanding and living by our own agenda. This selfishness keeps us consumed with our way, our priorities, and our understanding rather than God's.

Selfish self-love makes it difficult for us to consider the insights of others because we are too wrapped in our own. When seeing through the lens of selfish self-love, we will find ourselves using others to satisfy our own pleasure instead of loving others for God's pleasure. Selfish self-love can breed a sense of entitlement, leading us to demand what we want from others instead of asking respectfully for what we want and giving people the freedom to say no.

A person operating in self-preserving self-love will look after himself while also looking after others. For instance, if a husband gets hungry and plans to drive for some fast food, he would also check with his wife to see if she and the kids would like something. That way he could bring food home for them as well. Self-preserving self-love considers the interests of others as well as its own. When operating in self-preserving self-love, a person will pay the utility bills, buy clothes for himself, get regular medical check-ups, etc. However, he will also help others with their bills, get clothes for others where needed, drive others to the doctor when necessary to make sure they receive the care they need.

When operating in self-preserving self-love, a person will treat others the way he would want to be treated. The relationship will not be dominated by manipulation. For instance, he will not do for others to have them do something for him in return. We will do for others as we do for ourselves. We will truly be loving our neighbors as we love ourselves!

When a person is operating in soul-loving self-love, she will be learning and living out God's will in her life and with others. As she learns God's Word, she will be obedient to God and loving toward others as defined by God. Soul-loving self-love leads to a life of studying the Bible, listening to wise counsel, praying for wisdom, and allowing the Holy Spirit to illumine her mind with the truth—all for the purpose of living out truth in action before God and with others.

Where relationships are dominated by soul-loving self-love, we will see individuals who truly believe that the goal of God's instruction is to love from a pure heart, good conscience, and sincere faith. When we are operating in soul-loving self-love, we will find that the more we learn of God, the more we live by His standards and love others faithfully. We do not live to learn, but we learn to live. This process results in lives that are pleasing to God.

Our purpose here is to focus on the differences we can see in the three kinds of self-love: selfish, soul-preserving, and soul-loving. We have only touched on the ways these kinds of self-love affect our attitudes and treatment of others. However, an important biblical truth is that both soul-preserving and soul-loving self-love, when developed in our hearts and actions, will result in the ability to follow Christ's example of true sacrificial love for others.

SUMMARY

Selfish self-love can be defined as making self the priority for life or the central focus of existence. Self-preserving self-love can be defined as our natural tendency to take care of ourselves and preserve our material bodies. Soul-loving self-love can be defined as a person's effort to get wisdom and understanding so that he may live righteously.

Love for self is in an implied reality. The Bible affirms that we already love ourselves. We must learn to humble ourselves and start loving God and others more. The problems in our relationships are not caused by a lack of love for ourselves. The problems we face in our relationships are based on a lack of love for God and others. This is demonstrated in selfish self-love.

Self-preserving self-love and soul-loving self-love do not contradict or keep us from loving God and loving others. They will help us look out for others as we look out for ourselves, as well as get to know God better through wise counsel, praying for wisdom, and illumination of the Holy Spirit as we study His Word. Then we will find that we progress in living for God and loving others according to His Word. Whereas the world promotes self-love as a virtue to be learned, biblically we recognize self-love not as something to be learned but something already lived in a neutral (self-preserving self-love), wise (soul-loving self-love), or evil (selfish self-love) manner depending on the context. Therefore, self-love—instead of being part of the trinity of self-worship—can become part of the triangle of self-evaluation.

Chapter 7

PUTTING IT ALL TOGETHER

You've likely heard characters in a movie make this statement: "It's not you, it's me, and I just need to go and find myself!" As if they left themselves somewhere in the bushes or in some other city. This kind of talk causes so much confusion and disorder in people's lives. They are really dealing with an identity crisis. They lack understanding of who they are and how they are to govern themselves in relation to God and others. How we feel about ourselves, how we see ourselves, and how we look out for ourselves has more to do with our relationship to God and His will than it has to do with others. However, these issues do have a huge impact on our relationships with others.

Generally, when you hear the terms *self-esteem, self-image,* and *self-love,* they are all tied into one main concept. They are not presented as separate entities but as the same thing, either all bad or all good. On the contrary, we have been considering a different way to look at self-esteem, self-image, and self-love. We have examined a biblical alternative so that we will take a biblical perspective on how to handle matters pertaining to these issues.

Self-esteem should rightly be called conscience joy and conscience sorrow. It is a result and not a pursuit. Therefore, we Christians should be concentrating on loving God and loving others through the power of the Holy Spirit and not on improving our self-esteem.

As we love consistently, the result will be conscience joy. When we have unloving attitudes or do unloving actions, the result will be conscience sorrow.

Even though we are not to focus on improving our self-esteem, we are called to think soberly about ourselves (Rom. 12:3, Titus 2:12). This is where we understand the concept of self-image, which differs from conscience joy and conscience sorrow. Self-image is the evaluation of how a person sees his role and position in life. We are called to evaluate ourselves in light of what God says is true about us and not by our own opinions or the opinions of others.

Also, we need to understand that loving self is an implied reality that fits in three categories (selfish, self-preserving, or soul loving). Once we understand these categories of self-love, we will better understand what it means to deny ourselves. (See Genesis 4:6-7; Romans 12:1-3; Ephesians 5:28-29; and 1 Peter 1:13-15, 3:8-11.)

Let's see how these truths apply to some practical issues of life.

HUSBAND AND WIFE RELATIONSHIP

Want to revolutionize your relationship with your spouse? As we remember and apply what we've discussed thus far about self-esteem, we can see how these truths affect issues in our marriage. Our conscience joy and conscience sorrow are not determined by our spouse but by our choices. Our self-image should be based on God's Word and not the opinions of our spouse or of ourselves. We don't need to learn to love ourselves. As we gain a biblical understanding of who God is and what He commands, we will also learn who He says we are and are not. And in submission to God, we can begin to relate to and love our spouse in the beautiful way God has designed our marriages to flourish.

A CHILD AND "SELF-ESTEEM ISSUES"

Children who are experiencing what is termed "poor self-esteem" are really experiencing conscience sorrow. Whether child or adult, a person does not experience conscience sorrow due to his or her parents, other people, or circumstances of life. A child experiences conscience sorrow as a result of responding sinfully to parents, other people, or circumstances.

Therefore, the issue at hand is not how we help this child love herself more or believe in herself. On the contrary, how can we help the child see her sinful thoughts, words, or deeds in relation to parents, people, or circumstances? After taking care (with kindness and humility) to discover the problem, we are to help the child confess, repent of, and replace these sinful thoughts, words, or deeds with godly ones. The result will be conscience joy. If this child is an unbeliever, the process becomes an opportunity to present the gospel with anticipation of guiding the child into peace with God through salvation—an incredibly joyful experience for all.

We must note that since unbelievers and believers can experience conscience sorrow and conscience joy, if an unbeliever does what is right according to the work of the law written on his heart, he too can experience conscience joy (Rom. 2:14-15). Therefore, at the least we can help an unbelieving child see the error of his ways. This can be used as a redemptive opportunity by encouraging the child to understand that his sorrow is not tied to lack of love for or unbelief in himself, but ultimately to a sin choice he himself has made.

SPECIAL CONCERNS IN RELATION TO CHILDREN

We recognize that legitimate questions arise regarding the difficult situations in which some children begin their lives. We know that children are vulnerable to and indeed even molded in their view of themselves by their caregivers. Hopefully these are primarily their loving mothers and fathers, but sometimes a grandparent, foster parent, etc.

Sadly, some children are raised with incredibly warped views of themselves. They might consider themselves stupid, incapable, unlovable . . . all of the hideous negatives that are communicated or even beaten into them by evil or insane or substance-abusive people who should have loved and cared for them. So these children approach their lives with unbiblical views of themselves, resulting in their making bad decisions that create noisy souls.

Another aspect of this challenge is that some children, because they are born with physical or mental handicapping conditions, recognize that they can't do what they observe others doing. And whether anyone who takes care of them has this attitude or not, other children are often cruel in their responses to these specially challenged children. Children with handicaps can get the message: they are unacceptable to their peers. At certain stages of life, peer acceptance tends to be of biggest importance—far more even than a loving mom or dad saying they are great. So how do we address these matters? We know that Christ can transform our hearts, and we want to give hope and communicate truth to persons, whether child or adult, dealing with such hard realities.

First, we must understand that this is primarily an issue of self-image. Where children have been misused, abused, and told by words and/or actions that they are nothing or less than nothing, our first step is to demonstrate the love of Christ. Loving speech and appropriate actions that address basic physical needs and nurture can begin to provide a sense of comfort and stability to children.

Second, we begin to help children think in terms of biblical categories. This is done by replacing the mean and horrible things said to them with the biblically appropriate realities that God has made true to them through the Word of God. We would communicate that, unlike what some people have said or done to them, God has stated in His Word that you are created in His image and are fearfully and wonderfully made (Ps. 139:14). Of course, we speak in terms that the child can understand, such as changing "fearfully" to "amazingly" or "incredibly" if need be.

Third, when we believe the time is right, we begin to present the biblical meanings of *sinner, saint,* and *salvation.* We would help the children understand how these apply to every person and to themselves personally. Taking the time and patience to explain these realities at the level of their understanding without compromising the truth of God's Word, we would have the joy of leading children to grasp their own need for the gospel.

Fourth, we lead children to understand their limitations both physically and spiritually and that evil exists in the world. This is where we would guide children to understand how evil in the world can cause them to experience many bad and even cruel words and actions from others. Helping children understand what they can and cannot control, as well as how their choices and reactions to people and circumstances will be the driving force behind their feelings, can clarify their daily decisions to love or remain bitter.

We explain to them at the level they can understand how their choices and reactions to people and circumstances lead them to experience conscience joy and conscience sorrow. The goal is to teach these children that how they react and the choices they make in relation to the evil and negative things that happen to them will determine their feelings.

During this entire process, we continue to convey who God is: His love, expectations, support, and wisdom that He provides to us, knowing the limitations each of us have. We guide them into understanding who they are and who they are not, according to biblical categories as opposed to lies that were communicated to them. The goal is to teach them their need for Jesus Christ and His good news for them, in contrast to the evil that exists within each human and the world.

In summary, when children experience deep sorrow from the cruelty of others, we demonstrate the love of Jesus Christ to them. We guide them to see themselves in light of biblical categories (self-image). We describe to them how their actions and reactions to the world dictate the condition of their hearts (conscience joy/conscience sorrow). We show them who God is and why He created them and why they need Him. We help them to think biblically about themselves in light of their limitations. We introduce them to the gospel of Jesus Christ. While this process may not answer all the questions and implications tied to this complex matter, it can be a good start to see how this model can be applied.

UNDERSTANDING WHO WE ARE

A person will not have a right understanding of who he is if he does not come to embrace the reality of God's Word. Who we are is not determined by what we think of ourselves or how the world sees us. Who we are is completely determined by God. Therefore, if a person is to have right thinking about himself or a sober assessment of himself (Romans 12:3), he must look at himself in light of biblical categories. A person is either in Christ or in Adam, in darkness or in light, a Christian or an evildoer, a slave of God or slave of sin, etc. (Rom. 6:1-23, 1 Peter 4:15-16, Col. 1:13-14). A person must recognize and embrace his or her biological origin and function within the guidelines and guardrails of that origin as described and prescribed by God (Gen. 1:26–2:24). Moreover, he or she is to operate in light of being a servant of God who has been given spiritual gifts to serve the church (Rom. 12:3-8).

Therefore, as Christians growing toward maturity, we evaluate ourselves through this perspective. On the basis of Scripture, we must come to understand who we are and who we are not. For instance, the Bible says that a person in Christ has become a new creature—a newly created man or woman with a newly quickened spirit (2 Cor. 5:17). That means our position and condition have changed. We are no longer considered dead and hopeless sinners, but instead alive and saints in God's eyes. Then we are to be governed and guided by our identity and role as new creatures in Christ, not by our own ideas. This is an issue of self-image and not of conscience joy, conscience sorrow, or self-love. If we govern ourselves according to what God has described and prescribed, we will walk in humility. But pride leads to following our own opinions and the opinions of others.

HAVING CONFIDENCE IN OURSELVES?

We are not called to have confidence in ourselves or to believe in ourselves. The Bible warns us that he who trusts in his own heart is a fool (Prov. 28:26). We are called to recognize that our abilities are from God and to function within those abilities as prescribed and empowered by God (Rom. 12:3-8). As we walk according to God's commands, we will experience conscience joy and a confidence before God, knowing we are doing what pleases Him (1 John 3:21-22). You and I can have confidence, not so much in ourselves, but in God's empowerment of us to function as He has willed.

Having confidence in ourselves keeps the focus on self. However, functioning according to who we are commanded to be in Christ keeps us focused on God, resulting in experiencing a confidence in God rather than in self. This confidence assures our hearts that we are doing what is pleasing to God. This enables us to have confidence to draw ever nearer to Him (Prov. 28:1). Such confidence is not because of anything we can think, feel, or do, but it results from obedience to Christ.

Notice that this kind of confidence is very different from believing in yourself or seeking to feel good about yourself by accomplishing some goal. We can confidently embrace who we are commanded to be, acting in faith and experiencing conscience joy. This is where we see a biblical view of self-esteem (conscience joy) and a biblical view of self-image (humility) coming together.

PERSONAL RELATIONSHIPS WITH OTHERS

Because we aren't marooned on a deserted island, how we live each day affects many other people. Every word and action gives a glimpse of who we really are. We don't lack love for ourselves when we relate with others. We can either be preoccupied with self or fail to love others because of our selfish self-love. When we focus on how we are giving to others but not receiving in return, we are making ourselves the center of our giving to others. That is selfish self-love. It is understandable to want to receive from others, but it is not Christ-like to be consumed with receiving from others. Following His example means giving out love for others without focusing on receiving in return.

Each of our roles in life should be governed by the ordained design and prescribed will of God. If we have a role without a specific correlation in Scripture, we can examine that role's function. Is it a role calling us to lead, follow, serve, or fellowship with a person? Evaluate relevant Bible passages to determine how we are to lead, follow, serve, or fellowship with others. Any role we have that is antithetical to Christian standards and values should be discarded, since is it does not line up with how God has created us to be and to operate.

How we are treated by others does not determine our conscience joy or conscience sorrow, but how we treat people within the scope of our roles will determine our conscience joy or conscience sorrow.

Love of others and not love of self should determine how we communicate with and treat other people.

Self-esteem should rightly be called conscience joy and conscience sorrow. Christians should concentrate on loving God and loving others through the power of the Holy Spirit and not on improving their "self-esteem." As we love consistently, the result will be conscience joy. If we are unloving, the result will be conscience sorrow. Even though we are not to focus on improving our self-esteem, we are called to think soberly about ourselves, which introduces the concept of self-image. This differs from conscience joy and conscience sorrow. Self-image is the evaluation of how we see our roles and position in life. We are called to evaluate ourselves in light what God says is true about us and not by our own opinions or the opinions of others. Also, we need to understand that loving self is an implied reality that fits in three categories: selfish, self-preserving, or soul loving. Once we understand the categories of self-love, we will have a better understanding of what it means to deny ourselves. See the biblical bases for these ideas in Romans 2:14-16, Proverbs 28:1, Genesis 4:6-7, Romans 12:1-3, and Ephesians 5:28-29.

Our involvement with people and circumstances should be guided and guarded by these biblical principles instead of the secular humanistic values our culture brings to the table. According to Jim Owen, our prerequisite for love is not to understand and embrace ourselves but rather to develop an appreciation for how much we have been loved by God. In Owen's book *Christian Psychology's War on God's Word* (as referenced in Chapter 3), he states:

> Since the fall, the issue for mankind is not how we were
> made (in God's image) but what we have become. This issue is

not our self-esteem but our depravity. This issue is not what I am worth, but how can I become reconciled with God. My "created value" plays no role in such a confrontation. What matters is whether I am "in Christ". God created me in His image, but He is under no obligation to save me because of that, nor love me as He does. My sinful self is not a false self; it is what I am at birth. We are "by nature objects of wrath" (Ephesians 2:3) and will stay that way unless we are made new creations in Christ. When we seek to use the created value argument to deliberately bolster someone's self-esteem and claim it necessary and biblical to do so, because so many are racked with feelings of inferiority, we do a great disservice to the Gospel.

I pray that you have been helped to think through these issues. May God richly bless you to apply these insights and share them with others. And as this wonderful passage in 2 Peter 3:18 encourages us, may we all "grow in the grace and knowledge of our Lord and Savior Jesus Christ." As a result, we can trade the trinity of self-worship for the triangle of self-evaluation. "To Him be the glory, both now and to the day of eternity!"

Sources

CHAPTER I

Adler, Alfred. *The Science of Living.* New York: Routledge, 2013.

Biersdorf, John. "The Human Potential Movement and the Church." *Christianity and Crisis* 35, no. 4 (March 1975): 54-58.

Bowlby, John. *Maternal Care and Mental Health; A Report Prepared on Behalf of the World Health Organization as a Contribution to the United Nations Programme for the Welfare of Homeless Children.* 2nd ed. World Health Organization, Monograph series 2. Geneva: World Health Organization, 1952.

Bowlby, Richard. *Fifty Years of Attachment Theory.* London: Karnac on behalf of the Winnicott Clinic of Psychotherapy, 2004.

Branden, Nathaniel. *My Years with Ayn Rand.* San Francisco: Jossey-Bass, 1999.

———. *The Six Pillars of Self-Esteem.* New York: Bantam, 1994.

California Task Force to Promote Self-Esteem and Personal and Social Responsibility. *The Appendixes of Toward a State of Esteem.* Sacramento: California Department of Education, 1990.

Coopersmith, Stanley. *The Antecedents of Self-esteem.* London: Freeman, 1967.

Epstein, Seymour. *Cognitive-experiential Theory: An Integrative Theory of Personality.* New York: Oxford University Press, 2014.

Fenichel, Otto, and M. D. *The Psychoanalytic Theory of Neurosis.* New York: W.W. Norton, 1945.

Freud, Sigmund. *General Psychological Theory: Papers on Metapsychology.* Repr. New York: Touchstone, 1991.

Harrison, Glynn. *The Big Ego Trip: Rediscovering Grace in a Culture of Self-esteem*. Nottingham, England: Inter-Varsity, 2013.

Holifield, E. Brooks. *A History of Pastoral Care in America: From Salvation to Self-realization*. Nashville: Abingdon, 1983.

Horney, Karen. *Our Inner Conflicts, a Constructive Theory of Neurosis*. New York: W.W. Norton, 1945.

James, William. *The Principles of Psychology*, The Works of William James. Cambridge, MA: Harvard University Press, 1983.

Kernis, Michael H., ed. *Efficacy, Agency, and Self-esteem*. New York: Plenum Press, 1995.

Maslow, Abraham H. *Religions, Values, and Peak-Experiences*. Columbus: Ohio State University Press, 1964.

Maslow, Abraham. *Motivation and Personality*. Harper's Psychological Series. New York: Harper, 1954.

May, Rollo. *Power and Innocence*. New York: Norton, 1972.

Mecca, Andrew M., Neil J. Smelser, and John Vasconcellos, eds. *The Social Importance of Self-esteem*. Berkeley: University of California Press, 1989.

Meszaros, Katerina, and Stefan DeWalls. *Handbook on Psychology of Self-esteem*. Hauppauge, NY: Nova Science, 2011.

Mruk, Christopher J. *Self-esteem and Positive Psychology: Research, Theory, and Practice*. 4th ed. New York: Springer, 2013.

Oden, Thomas C. *Game Free; A Guide to the Meaning of Intimacy*. New York: Harper & Row, 1974.

Raschke, Carl A. "Human Potential Movement." *Theology Today* 33, no. 3 (October 1976): 253.

Rogers, Carl. *Client-centered Therapy: Its Current Practice, Implications, and Theory*. Boston: Houghton Mifflin, 1951.

———. *On Becoming a Person; A Therapist's View of Psychotherapy*. Boston: Houghton Mifflin, 1961.

Rosenberg, Morris. *Society and the Adolescent Self-image*. Princeton, NJ: Princeton University Press, 1965.

Tileaga, Cristian, Loughborough University, and Jovan By. *Psychology and*

History: Interdisciplinary Explorations. New York: Cambridge University Press, 2014.

Vitz, Paul C. *Psychology as Religion: The Cult of Self-worship.* 2nd ed. Carlisle, UK: Paternoster, 1994.

White, Robert. "Ego and Reality in Psychoanalytic Theory: A Proposal Regarding Independent Ego Energies." *Psychological Issues*, no. 3 (1963): 125-50.

Zeigler-Hill, Virgil, ed. *Self-esteem.* Current Issues in Social Psychology. New York: Psychology, 2013.

CHAPTER 2

Berg, Jim. *Changed into His Image: God's Plan for Transforming Your Life.* Greenville, SC: JourneyForth, 2017.

———. *Created for His Glory: God's Purpose for Redeeming Your Life.* Greenville, SC: BJU, 2002.

———. *Essential Virtues: Marks of the Christ-centered Life.* Greenville, SC: JourneyForth, 2008.

Boa, Kenneth, and Gail Burnett. *The Art of Living Well: A Biblical Approach from Proverbs.* Guidebook Series. Colorado Springs: NavPress, 1999.

Boa, Kenneth. *Conformed to His Image: Biblical and Practical Approaches to Spiritual Formation.* Grand Rapids: Zondervan, 2001.

Bridges, Jerry. *The Joy of Fearing God.* Colorado Springs: WaterBrook, 2016.

———. *True Community: The Biblical Practice of Koinonia.* Colorado Springs: NavPress, 2012.

Chafer, Lewis Sperry. *Systematic Theology Volume Seven.* Grand Rapids: Kregel, 1993.

Chester, Tim. *You Can Change: God's Transforming Power for Our Sinful Behavior and Negative Emotions.* Wheaton, IL: Crossway, 2010.

Erickson, Millard J. *Christian Theology.* 3rd ed. Grand Rapids: Baker Academic, 2013.

Fee, Gordon D. *Revelation: A New Covenant Commentary*. New Covenant Commentary Series. Cambridge, UK: Lutterworth, 2011.

Ferguson, Rick E. *The Servant Principle: Finding Fulfillment through Obedience to Christ*. Nashville: Broadman & Holman, 1999.

Ferguson, Sinclair B. *The Christian Life: A Doctrinal Introduction*. London: Hodder and Stoughton, 1981.

Fortune, Don and Katie. *Discover Your God-given Gifts*. Grand Rapids: Chosen, 2009.

Grudem, Wayne. *Making Sense of Salvation: One of Seven Parts*. Grand Rapids: Zondervan, 2011.

———. *Systematic Theology: An Introduction to Biblical Doctrine*. Grand Rapids: Zondervan, 1994.

Hendricks, William L. *The Doctrine of Man*. Nashville: Convention, 1977.

Hillis, Roger. *One Another Christianity: Restoring Life Changing Relationships in the Church*. Bowling Green, KY: One Stone, 2018.

Hull, Bill. *The Complete Book of Discipleship: On Being and Making Followers of Christ*. Colorado Springs: NavPress, 2006.

Koessler, John. *True Discipleship: The Art of Following Jesus*. Chicago: Moody, 2003.

Lane, Tim, and Paul Tripp. *Relationships: A Mess Worth Making*. Greensboro, NC: New Growth, 2008.

Lightner, Robert P. *Handbook of Evangelical Theology: A Historical, Biblical, and Contemporary Survey and Review*. Grand Rapids: Kregel, 1995.

———. *Sin, the Savior, and Salvation: The Theology of Everlasting Life*. Nashville: T. Nelson, 1991.

MacArthur, John, ed. *Think Biblically! Recovering a Christian Worldview*. Wheaton, IL: Crossway, 2009.

MacArthur, John. *Christ's Call, Our Response: Follow Me*. Nashville: J. Countryman, 2004.

———. *Good News: The Gospel of Jesus Christ*. Orlando: Reformation Trust, 2018.

Moo, Douglas J. *James: An Introduction and Commentary*, Tyndale New Testament Commentaries. Downers Grove, IL: InterVarsity, 2009.

Ogden, Greg. *Transforming Discipleship: Making Disciples a Few at a Time*. Downers Grove, IL: InterVarsity, 2003.

Packer, J. I. *Knowing God*. Downers Grove, IL: InterVarsity, 1993.

Patterson, Paige. *Revelation: An Exegetical and Theological Exposition of Holy Scripture: New American Commentary*. Nashville: Holman, 2012.

Peterson, Robert A. *Salvation Accomplished by the Son: The Work of Christ*. Wheaton, IL: Crossway, 2012.

Piper, John. *A Peculiar Glory: How the Christian Scriptures Reveal Their Complete Truthfulness*. Wheaton, IL: Crossway, 2016.

———. *Future Grace: The Purifying Power of the Promises of God*. Colorado Springs: Multnomah, 2012.

———. *God's Passion for His Glory: Living the Vision of Jonathan Edwards, with the Complete Text of the End for Which God Created the World*. Wheaton, IL: Crossway, 1998.

Ryken, Philip Graham. *Jeremiah and Lamentations: From Sorrow to Hope*. Wheaton, IL: Crossway Books, 2001.

———. *The Message of Salvation: By God's Grace, for God's Glory*. Downers Grove, IL: InterVarsity, 2001.

Ryrie, Charles Caldwell. *Basic Theology: A Popular Systemic Guide to Understanding Biblical Truth*. Chicago: Moody, 1999.

Stott, John R. W. *Basic Christianity*. Downers Grove, IL: IVP Books, 2008.

Thomson, Rich. *The Heart of Man and the Mental Disorders: How the Word of God Is Sufficient, a Distinctly Christian Approach*. Alief, TX: Biblical Counseling Ministries, 2012.

Tozer, A. W. *The Knowledge of the Holy: The Attributes of God: Their Meaning in the Christian Life*. New York: HarperSanFrancisco, 1992.

Wiersbe, Warren W. *The Bible Exposition Commentary Volume 1*. Colorado Springs: Victor, 2001.

CHAPTER 3

Adams, Jay E. *The Biblical View of Self-esteem, Self-love, Self-image.* Eugene, OR: Harvest House, 1986.

Almy, Gary L. *How Christian Is Christian Counseling? The Dangerous Secular Influences That Keep Us from Caring for Souls.* Wheaton, IL: Crossway Books, 2000.

Almy, Gary, and Carol Tharp Almy. *Addicted to Recovery.* Eugene, OR: Harvest House, 1994.

Babler, John, David Penely, and Mike Bizzell. *Counseling by the Book.* Maitland, FL: Xulon, 2007.

Bonhoeffer, Dietrich. *The Cost of Discipleship.* New York: Macmillan, 1959.

Bulkley, Ed. *Why Christians Can't Trust Psychology.* Eugene, OR: Harvest House, 1993.

Guinness, Os, and John Seel, eds. *No God but God: Breaking with the Idols of Our Age.* Chicago: Moody, 1992.

Owen, Jim. *Christian Psychology's War on God's Word: The Victimization of the Believer.* Santa Barbara, CA: EastGate, 2003.

Tyler, David. *Jesus Christ: Self-Denial or Self-Esteem?* Bemidji, MN: Focus, 2014.

CHAPTERS 4-6

Adams, Jay E. *The Christian Counselor's Manual: The Practice of Nouthetic Counseling.* The Jay Adams Library. Grand Rapids: Zondervan, 1973.

Boa, Kenneth. *Conformed to His Image: Biblical and Practical Approaches to Spiritual Formation.* Grand Rapids: Zondervan, 2001.

Davis, Andrew M. *An Infinite Journey: Growing Toward Christlikeness.* Greenville, SC: Ambassador International, 2014.

Edwards, Dwight. *Revolution Within: A Fresh Look at Supernatural Living.* Colorado Springs: WaterBrook, 2001.

Ferguson, Sinclair B. *The Christian Life: A Doctrinal Introduction*. London: Hodder and Stoughton, 1981.

Gilbert, Greg. *What Is the Gospel?* 9Marks Series. Wheaton, IL: Crossway, 2010.

Jaeggli, Randy. *More Like the Master: Reflecting the Image of God*. Greenville, SC: Ambassador, 2004.

Leedy, Randy. *Love Not the World: Winning the War against Worldliness*. Greenville, SC: Bob Jones University Press, 2012.

Machen, J. Gresham. *The Christian View of Man*. London: Banner of Truth Trust, 1965.

Mahaney, C. J. *How Can I Change? Victory in the Struggle against Sin*. Gaithersburg, MD: Sovereign Grace Ministries, 1993.

Murray, Andrew. *Humility: The Beauty of Holiness*. American ed., rev. Fort Washington, PA: Christian Literature Crusade, 2006.

Whitney, Donald S. *Spiritual Disciplines within the Church: Participating Fully in the Body of Christ*. Colorado Springs: NAVPress, 2014.

Willard, Dallas. *The Divine Conspiracy: Rediscovering Our Hidden Life in God*. San Francisco: HarperSanFrancisco, 1998.

Wuest, Kenneth S. *Wuest's Word Studies from the Greek New Testament: For the English Reader*, vol. 2. Grand Rapids, MI: Eerdmans, 1997.

About the Author

Dr. Nicolas André Ellen is the Senior Pastor of Community of Faith Bible Church in Houston, TX, and Senior Professor of Biblical Counseling at the College of Biblical Studies in Houston. He has also developed a biblical counseling training center, Expository Counseling Training Center LLC.

He received a B.A. in Business Administration from the University of Houston; M.A. in Christian Education from Dallas Theological Seminary; M.A. in Biblical Counseling from The Masters University, Santa Clarita, CA; D.Min. with a concentration in Biblical Counseling from Southern Baptist Theological Seminary, Louisville, KY; and Ph.D. in Biblical Counseling from Southwestern Baptist Theological Seminary, Fort Worth, TX.

Dr. Ellen is a Certified Biblical Counselor and also a Fellow with the Association of Certified Biblical Counselors (ACBC). He travels nationwide with the organization teaching biblical counseling principles. Dr. Ellen and his wife, Dr. Venessa Ellen, have two children and four grandchildren.

CPSIA information can be obtained
at www.ICGtesting.com
Printed in the USA
BVHW070350200322
631660BV00008B/1296